'63

The Story of the 1963
World Champion
Chicago Bears

1963 Chicago Bears team picture. Courtesy of Chicago Bears.

The Story of the 1963
World Champion
Chicago Bears

Gary Youmans *and* Maury Youmans

Campbell Road Press, Inc.

To Our Parents

We honor and dedicate this book to their memory

for teaching us the meaning of self-sacrifice

and unselfish love.

There was always an extra plate at the table for a friend.

May that lesson never be lost.

That 1963 team was the best football team without question that George Halas ever coached. When George Halas hired me in 1982, he had one request. 'I want you to bring this thing back to what it was in '63.' I told him I didn't know if we can get those kind of players . . . but if we can . . . we will have the same attitude and zeal that those guys had. I promised him that."

—MIKE DITKA
Tight End

Gary Youmans grew up in Syracuse, New York, where he developed his longstanding love of sports. After playing basketball at Ashland College in Ohio, he went on to coach high school basketball in Florida and professional basketball in the Continental Basketball Association (CBA) and in Canada. He has even owned a minor league basketball team. Now a sports marketing consultant, Youmans has returned to the Syracuse area, where he was raised.

Maury Youmans is a Syracuse University graduate and was a member of the 1959 Syracuse University Football Team. He was named to the 1960 College All-Star Team and went on to play defensive end for the Chicago Bears and Dallas Cowboys, retiring in 1965 after six years in the NFL. Appointed by Governor Bob Martinez to serve on the first Florida Sports Foundation Board, he later became its chairman. Youmans was for many years on the selection committee for the Hall of Fame Bowl, now known as the Outback Bowl. He is president of Youmans Consulting Group. He and his wife, Betty, reside in St. Pete Beach, Florida, and summer on Wellesley Island, New York. They have three children and five grandchildren.

Contents

Preface

GARY YOUMANS

Writing this book was a wonderful look back in time. The Chicago Bears in 1963 were a very special team with a most interesting array of characters. I found their reflections on that remarkable season fascinating, especially their candid recollections of team owner and coach George Halas. Most described their relationship with Halas as one of both love and hate. Papa Bear was a tough man to deal with, but his total dedication to his sport won him the undying respect of everyone. We tried to present an honest inside look at this true giant of the game. His many sides come out as the '63 story unfolds—some good, some bad, many comical.

Without the efforts of my brother, who conducted all the interviews with his teammates and coaches, this book would not have been written. I am indebted to him and all the 1963 Chicago Bears for allowing us to share their memories of that wonderful championship season.

Acknowledgments

MAURY YOUMANS

Sharing the highlights of our 1963 season was difficult for me. Unfortunately, I was to miss the whole season because of a knee injury that occurred in the second exhibition game, against the Washington Redskins. Under normal conditions I would have returned to action within six weeks, but it was not to be. After the operation an infection set in that did not clear up until the Los Angeles Rams game on November 10. George Allen told me I would be activated the following week, replacing John Johnson. In beating the Rams, John received the game ball for his outstanding play. Needless to say, they decided to keep a healthy John Johnson on the roster.

On the plus side I got the chance to share the memories of a special season with my teammates and coaches, who together made it happen. My thanks to them for bringing to life a special season in our lives. I want to thank the Chicago Bears for all their cooperation in making this book a reality. I especially want to thank Dan Uska for his extra efforts in providing us with the team photos and to Chuck Burkett for all his help. Finally, as always, a big thanks to the folks at Syracuse University Press, who provided us with so much help in putting this book together.

The authors of this book are personally responsible for all errors of omission and commission, misstatements, inaccuracies, and embellishments. In telling this story, if it's wrong, it's our error.

'63

The Story of the 1963
World Champion
Chicago Bears

Bears getting ready to do battle. *Left to right:* Bob Kilcullen (74), Johnny Morris (47), Joe Marconi (34), Doug Atkins (81), Billy Martin (22), Earl Leggett (71), Ed O'Bradovich (87), and Bill George (61). Courtesy of Ron Nelson/Prairie Street Art.

1

The Old Zipperoo

On a warm spring day in 1963, George Halas sat in his office talking football with his young defensive coordinator, George Allen. Halas's Chicago Bears had a record of 9–5 in 1962, but two crushing defeats to the Green Bay Packers had soured the old man's thoughts of that season. It had been seventeen years since the Bears had won the title, and Halas was sick of hearing about how great Vince Lombardi and his World Champion Packers were. The old coach was not going to leave any stone unturned this year in his drive to beat his archenemy, Lombardi.

Halas finished straightening some papers on his desk, pushed his chair back, and began. "George, in your opinion how good is our defense? Now, before you answer me, I want to make this clear: I want the truth, no whitewash job, for heaven sake, no bullshit! Are we as good as we think we are?"

George Allen, sitting in front of Halas with his legs crossed, quickly glanced at his notes, then up at Halas with a slight smile on his face. "Coach, on paper we have the best group coming to training camp that I have seen since I have been with you. The competition for starting positions will be strong. We will separate the wheat from the chaff, but this will give us good depth at all positions. If we can stay healthy, we will be very good. I've spoken to the players, and they all have promised to report in good shape. They recognize how important that is. Bill George told me last night he's ready to kick some ass. Bill told me he feels our team will be much better with a simple 4–3 defense, rather than the multiple sets Shaughnessy used the past couple of years. He felt it has been too confusing for many of the players."

Halas smiled; he had great confidence in Allen. The young coach was a bright, articulate man. He had been a big asset to the Chicago Bears on and off the field, battling the upstart AFL for players. Allen had proven to be a master recruiter. Handsome and upbeat, George Allen would do anything to win; the old man liked that. Finishing second was not the creed of George Halas, and he wanted people who transcended his thinking. George Allen was that kind of person. Halas's approach to football was hard, no-nonsense. Get the job done, take no prisoners. Allen was more of a motivator. He kept the players up and focused on the positive. He was very analytical, a good balance to Halas's crustiness. They worked well together. Halas had high hopes for this young coach. He felt he could trust him.

Clark Shaughnessy had abruptly departed the Bears in the middle of the previous season, after a disagreement with Halas. Shaughnessy, a legend in coaching, was credited with being the first college coach to use the T formation. Initially an offensive coach with the Bears, he had been in charge of the defense the past few years. Time had taken its toll on him. He would get confused during games and agitated over the least little thing. Players were getting frustrated with his defensive schemes, and it had become apparent to Halas that some of the defensive talent was not being used properly. Shaughnessy's departure and Allen's appointment to the top spot had been positive moves for the team.

ROOSEVELT TAYLOR (Defensive Back): "Clark Shaughnessy was easily a genius of football. I was the reason he left the Bears. He was attempting to do something new in pro football and send in the safety blitz. Halas told him, 'We need Rosie back there covering men out of the backfield. We can't have him running after the quarterback.' Clark said, 'Well, George, you have me as the defensive coordinator. Seems like if I think it is good for the team, I have the right to put it in.' The old man says, 'Clark, we can't do that.' Clark told him if he didn't

Clark Shaughnessy. © 1960 by Laughead Photographers, courtesy of Chicago Bears.

put in the safety blitz, he quit, and walked out. George Allen took over, and a short time later we had the safety blitz."

MAURY YOUMANS (Defensive End): "Clark Shaughnessy liked to control everything. His defensive schemes were very complicated, and probably that's why Halas had George Allen as Shaughnessy's as-

Roosevelt Taylor. Courtesy of Chicago Bears.

sistant. Allen could report back to the old man and tell him what was going on with the defense. On one play I would line up inside the tackle; the next time I might be split way out to the left. He had color schemes for all his formations, like 'Blue dot dash cherry go.' It was not an easy system to understand or play under."

Allen was installing a basic 4–3 defense. The young coach felt that up front the Bears would be outstanding. Led by Doug Atkins and tackle Stan Jones, the core group of Fred Williams, Earl Leggett, Bob

Kilcullen, Ed O'Bradovich, and Maury Youmans provided experienced front-line players. Allen recognized that if he could eliminate the players jumping around, and concentrated more on creating a better pass rush, this group would excel. At least he thought this would happen. The linebackers with veteran Bill George in the middle were also very good. Larry Morris and Joe Fortunato were mobile, hard-nosed players who as bookends to George could roam sideline to sideline making plays.

In the defensive backfield Roosevelt Taylor, Richie Petitbon, and Dave Whitsell were tough guys who came to play every day. Longtime Bear J. C. Caroline was slowly being eased out by Bennie McRae, but still provided quality play at the corner position and with the special teams. Allen was confident he could build a strong unit out of all this talent.

STAN JONES (Defensive Tackle): "George Halas never did know what the defenses were when Clark Shaughnessy was defensive coordinator. That would get Shaughnessy in trouble, because he wouldn't tell him who was playing well and who wasn't. Halas would tell him, 'Hey, Clark, I'm paying these guys. I want to know who is doing their job and who is not doing their job, but I don't know your defenses.' Allen's system brought accountability to the defense."

DOUG ATKINS (Defensive End): "At defensive end I could beat most tackles, but Shaughnessy had me going out and covering passes on some plays. Sometimes I would go a whole game and never make a tackle. When we would look at the film, he didn't know whether to chew me out or not, because he didn't know himself what defense we were in. It was Mickey Mouse, with players jumping all over the place. It needed to be simplified. That's why George Allen was such a big part of our success."

George Allen was about to continue his critique of the defense when Halas's secretary broke in on the intercom. "Mr. Halas, you have a call on line one. It's Coach Lombardi. He said it is important."

"What the hell does he want?" growled the old man. "Every time he calls he pretends like we're good friends, always asking how I'm feeling, like I'm sick or something. He's always trying to screw me in a trade. He's so 'Holier than Thou.' I hate talking to him." Halas grabbed the phone.

"Vince, how are you? I have been so busy I haven't had a chance to talk with you and congratulate you on the championship. No, I'm fine. Thanks for asking. What can I do for you? . . . A trade—hell, the way you handled us last year, I wouldn't think you would want any of our players. Go on, Vince, what have you got in mind? . . . Oh, you have some interest in acquiring another defensive player. Anyone in particular, or would you like the whole damn lot of them? No, there's a few we plan on keeping. What are you proposing? I understand we're just talking . . . exploring ideas . . . but there must be a particular player you're interested in? . . . I see . . . you're considering adding a defensive end. . . . Who are you considering trading? . . . Oh, you're not sure . . . I see . . . possibly giving up draft picks or some cash. Well, Vince, I can tell you first off Doug Atkins isn't going anywhere and Ed O'Bradovich we like a lot. Maury Youmans has been here for three years and played some good football for us. We wouldn't be interested in draft picks for those young men, and I can assure you the Chicago Bears don't need money. I'm not saying we couldn't use more money with the high salaries today. Hell, we had to give a rookie a $2,500 bonus just to sign him. Competing against that damn AFL is wrecking the game. At this time, Vince, we would only consider trading a player for another player. . . . Yes, I understand we're just talking, and I will discuss our conversation with my staff. . . . No, Vince, I wouldn't rule out anything. Thanks for calling. . . . What's that? . . . No, I'm feeling great, but again thanks for your concern about my well-being. I can assure you I will see you down the line. Good-bye, Vince."

Halas slammed down the phone. "He's always conniving, that guy. He wants our players but doesn't want to give up anything. What bullshit! I should have told him I'll give him $500 for Jerry Kramer, or $1,000 for Jim Taylor, or two draft picks for Bart Starr. The gall of that guy. I want to kick his ass. We're not letting them get the best of us this year."

Seeing the old man's frustration, Allen piped in. "We'll get him this year, Coach. This year we will be ready for them."

Bill Wade. Courtesy of Chicago Bears.

Halas nodded his approval. "You're right, George, we have the desire this year, the mental toughness it takes to win. We'll give them the old zipperoo."

The Green Bay Packers had done a number on the Bears in 1962. After opening the season with two straight wins over the 49ers and the Rams, the Bears were thumped by the Packers 49–0 in Green Bay. The return match five weeks later at Wrigley Field wasn't much better, as the Packers beat the Bears 38–7. The Bears would lose only three more games during the rest of the season and closed out the 1962 year with wins over the Rams (30–14) and the Lions (3–0).

This year Halas was determined to challenge Green Bay for the title. Led by veteran quarterback Bill Wade, the offense had averaged 22.9 points per game last season. Wade had thrown for 18 touchdowns but had been intercepted 24 times. An area of concern was Wade being sacked 27 times. Halas knew his offensive line had to do a better job protecting the quarterback. Backup quarterback Rudy Bukich had also proven to be a very capable player. He was an accurate passer, and all the coaches and players had great confidence in him. A few players felt the offense might even be more explosive with Bukich as quarterback. Bukich would come to training camp this year planning to compete hard for the starting position.

ANGELO COIA (Flanker): "We had two great passers with the Bears in 1963. Bill Wade could throw the ball on a hook-and-out better than anyone. I watch the guys today, and there's nobody that can throw the ball any better than Bill Wade. He was a very accurate passer, and he was a tough guy. Rudy Bukich had an unbelievably strong arm and threw the hardest ball I have ever seen. I remember he always wanted to bet that he could stand on the 50-yard line of Wrigley Field and throw the ball out of the stadium. Nobody would bet him."

The two Chicago quarterbacks had a fine group of receivers to throw to in 1963, starting with Mike Ditka. "Iron Mike" had established himself in his first two seasons with the Bears as the premier tight end in football. Voted rookie of the year in 1961, Ditka's no-nonsense approach to winning football games was contagious among his teammates. Flanker Johnny Morris was also a fine receiver and had caught 47 passes for two touchdowns last season. Originally drafted as a running back in 1958, this outstanding athlete was now being used exclusively as a flanker. Fourth-year pro John Farrington provided a big target opposite Mike Ditka at left end. Farrington had the size and speed to be a very good player but still dropped too many passes. He needed to be much more consistent this year in order to gain the confidence of his quarterbacks. Fleet-footed Angelo Coia, out of Southern

Cal, provided the Bears with their deep threat. An alternate on the 1960 Olympic track team, Coia had caught 22 passes for four touchdowns in 1962. Averaging a team-leading 16.4 yards per catch, he rounded out a very good group of receivers.

BILL WADE (Quarterback): "I thought Johnny Morris was a great football player. Without any question I felt there were times when he could get clear against anybody in the business. One time I called for him to run an up. Johnny says, 'I'm not going to run an up anymore.' I said, 'Johnny we got to figure this out.' We were at practice, and I asked him why he wouldn't run an up. He said, 'I'm just not going to run an up anymore.' I said, 'Well, how about a wiggle up?' He would go down and wiggle right before he would accelerate past the defensive halfback. He wouldn't run it straight up or peel out; he'd go down and make a little wiggle move and go. So we put in a wiggle up, and he would run a wiggle up. It worked well. It helped to set up the comeback inside. When he started making the little wiggle, the guy didn't know what the heck to think. Johnny would do a comeback and be wide open. He was a super pass receiver. Johnny Morris wasn't afraid to block. He would block those big guys, as little as he was. He weighed 180 pounds."

The team's depth at running backs provided George Halas with a number of options and question marks going into the 1963 season. Fullback Rick Casares, a tough, dependable back over the years, had been banged up the previous season, and was being challenged by Joe Marconi for playing time. Marconi, who had come over to the Bears from the Rams following the 1961 season, was proving to be a very good addition to the Bears' ball-controlled offense.

The Bears' fleet-footed running back Willie Galimore had been injured most of 1962, and was returning after knee surgery. In Galimore's absence, rookie Ronnie Bull had played well. The former Baylor All American had gained 363 yards rushing and caught 31 passes for three touchdowns. Lacking Galimore's elusiveness, Bull was a strong runner, especially between the tackles, and proved to be a very capable receiver as well. Because of Bull's strong play the previous season, Halas decided he would bring Galimore along slowing in training camp. As the regular season progressed the Bears could use Galimore's talents, so there was no sense of urgency to have him play in the preseason.

BILL WADE (Quarterback): "Willie Galimore was just coming around as a great pass receiver in 1963. When I first got to the Bears, he could hardly catch a pass. He would slap at it like he was slapping flies. He had never been taught how to properly catch a ball, but he was getting where I could send him downfield and there was no linebacker on earth that was going to cover him. When we would split him out to the left by himself, the defense would be forced to put the free safety on his side. That meant that on the other side, Johnny [Morris] and Mike [Ditka] were in man-to-man coverage."

ANGELO COIA (Flanker): "Rick Casares was a rare guy. He was 6'3", 240 pounds—and he could run. He was like the backs are today. I remember one year we were playing an exhibition game. He ran the ball off tackle, and he says, 'Hey, Ang, I think I broke my ribs.' I said, 'You broke your ribs?' He says, 'Yeah, I think so.' The next play they throw a screen pass, and he gains seven yards and gets a first down. He goes out of the game, and he has two broken ribs. Some people can't even breathe with a broken rib, and he's playing football. Rick was a tough guy. I heard Mike Ditka once say on TV that the toughest guys he ever met in football were Doug Atkins and Rick Casares."

STAN JONES (Defensive Tackle): "Rick Casares was way ahead of his time. He would come back in the huddle and say, 'Man give me the ball, I feel the vibes.' We weren't into that 'hip' talk at that time. What the hell is he talking . . . 'the vibes'? He was a tough guy, though. He would play hurt. Rick would have been a great tight end. I don't think he ever dropped a pass. Toward the end of his career he could have been a hell of a tight end."

George Allen and Halas continued discussing the team for the rest of the afternoon. Each man knew the importance of the approaching season. The Bears had the talent to compete, but the opportunities to win a championship with this group were diminishing with each passing season. Age was starting to catch up with some of the veteran players, many of whom were near the end of their careers. Halas wanted his beloved Bears back on top. Somehow he would have them ready. He was a man who was used to getting his way.

RICHIE PETITBON (Defensive Back): "I thought when George Allen took over it was a good move. Clark was a genius, but he was so smart that most of us didn't know what the hell was going on. George simplified things, and we obviously had a lot of talent on that team. I think it made all the difference in the world. George got Doug Atkins to play. He was fabulous that year."

Chuck MATHER

BACKFIELD COACH

When I first came to the Bears as a young coach, Halas put me as Clark Shaughnessy's assistant. In the first meetings I was taking notes. Clark went to Halas and said, 'Mather's copying down all my stuff, and I don't want anybody knowing my stuff.' So Halas moved me to offense.

"George Allen had gotten fired out with the Rams when Sid Gilman took over. Allen was working with the sporting goods company Voit. They had this weighted football that would supposedly strengthen a quarterback's arm. Anyway, Allen was going around to the different pro teams introducing this weighted football. When he got to the Bears he asked me to get him an interview with Halas, which I did. Halas of course didn't buy any weighted footballs from him.

"Two weeks later I received this nice two-page letter from Allen thanking me for helping him. He went on to say how lucky I was to be working in the NFL, especially with George Halas. He said he hoped he would get another chance himself someday. I really appreciated the letter, and I felt sorry for George not being able to coach.

"Later on, before our game with Los Angeles, I mentioned to Halas about bringing Allen in to tell us about the Rams. He had coached there and probably could help us in our preparation to play them. Halas said that was a good idea, and we brought Allen in. After a few days Halas says to me, 'Get him the hell out of here!' At that time we had just lost our player-personnel guy, who had passed away. I said to Halas that Allen knows a lot of college coaches, why not have him take over as player-personnel director? Halas said okay and George came in and did a great job for us. The players he brought to the Bears were the players that won a championship for us, but he always wanted to coach. Shaughnessy didn't want him but finally in 1961 agreed to have him as his assistant. When Shaughnessy left in 1962 Allen took over. He did well because he always presented a good game plan. He broke film down and was always prepared. The players immediately responded to his coaching style."

George Halas. Courtesy of Chicago Bears.

2

George Halas

*In the early 1960s, the Bears, trailing by two points
late in the game, were moving down the field. Facing
a fourth and inches, Coach George Halas decided to
kick a field goal. As the ball was snapped, one of the
Bears' offensive linemen slipped, allowing his man to
shoot into the backfield and block the kick. Throwing
his arms up in disgust, the old man sprinted onto the
field where he kicked and cursed the offensive lineman all the way to the bench. In a booming voice you
could hear halfway around Wrigley Field, Halas
berated the offending lineman, challenging his
manhood, his intelligence, and threatening to cut
him off the team right on the spot. Such was the life of
a player who drew the ire of Papa Bear. No one was
off limits, and Halas, with his famous temper, could
make it personal. The man did not like to lose.*

In 1920 A. E. Staley, president of the Staley Starch Works in Decatur,
Illinois, asked George Halas to come into his office. Halas, who had
been hired the year before as a chemical engineer, also was the coach of
the company baseball and football teams. An outstanding end at Illinois, he had culminated his college career by winning the Most Valuable Player Award in the 1919 Rose Bowl. Halas, who had a pipeline to

recruit top players for the Staley teams, had incurred problems in scheduling reliable opponents who would actually show up for the games. Staley had made a sizable financial commitment to fund these recreational programs, even agreeing to Halas's demands that the team practice on company time. He wanted to see some type of league formed that would ensure legitimate opponents to compete against. He wanted to see the whole thing better organized.

Halas knocked on the door and walked in. Staley, sitting at his big mahogany desk, motioned him to a wooden chair in front of the desk. "George, I want to talk with you about an idea I got. There's a meeting in Canton, Ohio, on September 20, regarding a professional football league. I want you to represent the Staley Starch Works at that meeting."

Young George moved forward in his chair. He had heard about this proposed league and had planned to talk with Staley about it. "Yes, sir," Halas answered. Clearing his throat, he added, "I would be honored to represent your company, Mr. Staley. I think it's time something like this was organized. I will be happy to go to Canton. I have some ideas on how it should be set up."

Staley nodded his head in approval. It had gotten back to him that Halas had been talking about a professional league for months. Occasionally Staley had to remind his young employee that this was a Starch company, not just a place for former college athletes to hang out and play ball. Halas had done everything Staley had asked of him. He was a hard worker. Staley just didn't want his young coach to get out of control. "Good, George. It's all set. You will go to Canton on the twentieth. That's all."

Halas's feet hardly touched the ground as he left Staley's office. A professional football league, and he, George Halas, would be a part of it. This was a dream come true.

On September 20, 1920, at a meeting in Canton, Ohio, the Staley Starch Works became a charter member of the American Professional Football League. The franchise fee was one hundred dollars. Twelve teams were awarded franchises, and the board of directors appointed the biggest name in sports, Jim Thorpe, as the league's first president.

George Halas was ecstatic about being part of this new league. In his eyes, its potential was limitless.

On his return from Canton, the rookie coach/player went right to work recruiting the team, continuing to recommend to Staley outstanding employees who also happened to be football players. In the inaugural season, Halas saw his team finish second, with a record of 5–1–2. Staley was overjoyed with the results on the field, but the cost of funding a football team was far more than he had imagined. Finally, in 1921, he told his coach that the Staley Starch Works could no longer support a professional football team. Staley loved Halas, he saw the potential of professional football, but he could no longer commit the financial resources the team required. He had a business that needed his full attention. Staley would miss being involved in the games and the publicity his company received from it, but it was time to move aside. Staley felt an obligation to his fellow owners, so rather than disband the team or put it up for sale, he made Halas an offer he couldn't refuse. He would give the team to him with one stipulation: that he move the team to Chicago. Staley sweetened the deal by giving Halas five thousand dollars for operating capital, but Halas had to agree to keep the Staley name for one year. The two men shook hands and the deal was done.

Halas's first order of business on arriving in Chicago was finding a place to play. He first approached Bill Veeck, owner of the Chicago Cubs, about playing home games at Cubs Park (Wrigley Field). Veeck liked the idea of having a tenant, creating another source of income, especially in the fall when there was no baseball. The two men quickly put a deal together. Veeck doubted this sport would catch on like baseball, but the extra money would come in handy. Chicago's new professional football team now had a place to call home.

In 1921 the Chicago Staleys finished first in the league, with a record of 9–1–1. Following that first season, Halas renamed the team the Chicago Bears. Halas was a Cubs fan and had great respect for Bill Veeck, so, playing off the Cubs' name, he decided on the Bears. Football, being a rough-and-tumble sport, needed a more manly name than the Cubs. The Chicago Bears was a perfect name.

The Bears struggled in the early years in Chicago to find their fan base. In 1925 the opportunity to achieve credibility and attract fans finally arrived. The Bears signed Red Grange, the greatest player in college football. Every team in the league had been after Grange's services, but Halas, the shrewd businessman, had a plan. Halas had worked diligently behind the scenes with local theater owner C. C. Pyle. The two men concocted a plan to take the Bears on a tour, with Grange as the star attraction. Pyle's part in this scheme was to convince Grange to sign a contract to play for the Bears. Halas's part was to fund the tour. Both men, after much haggling, agreed to split the gate receipts down the middle. The barnstorming tour would net Grange one hundred thousand dollars.

Pyle sprang into action following Red Grange's last college game. First, a secret meeting was arranged, where Pyle presented Grange with the plan that would make him one hundred thousand dollars. The Bears would play ten games in eighteen days, with the tour beginning in Chicago with a game against the Chicago Cardinals. All Grange had to do was make Pyle his agent, and sign a contract with the Chicago Bears. Grange agreed.

On November 26, 1925, thirty-six thousand spectators turned out to watch Red Grange's professional debut, a record attendance for professional football at that time. When the tour finished up at the Polo Grounds, before seventy thousand screaming fans, more than two hundred thousand people had witnessed the exhibition games. Most were there to see Red Grange, not professional football, but the impact of the large crowds caught the attention of the elite sportswriters of the day. Grantland Rice, Damon Runyon, and Westbrook Pegler began following the tour, giving this new sport the national publicity it needed to survive and grow. The success of the tour prompted Halas to create a second tour, this time beginning in the South, then proceeding to the West Coast. On this tour the Bears would play nine games in thirty-eight days. Again the games attracted large crowds, with more than seventy thousand people turning out to watch the Bears play at the L.A. Coliseum. Halas had achieved all he could ask for from the two tours: credibility with the sportswriters and a new fan base to build on. Red Grange became a rich man.

George Halas retired as a player and coach in 1930, but he contin-

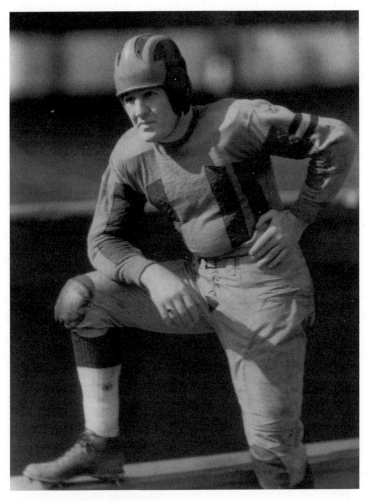

Red Grange. © Brace Photo.

ued to work to make pro football a popular sport. Concerned about teams trying to sign players who still had college eligibility left, the Bears owner pushed through a rule prohibiting NFL teams from signing players who hadn't graduated.

In 1936 the NFL instituted a college draft. Each team would draft nine players from the crop of graduating seniors. The idea of a draft had been kicked around for years. Bert Bell, owner of the Philadelphia Eagles, had introduced the idea in the early 1930s. Bell's reasoning was that by having only one team bid for a player's services, the owners would be able to keep player salaries down. This caught the attention of all the owners, including George Halas. If the system held true, then the league would have parity, and chronic losers such as Bell's team, the Philadelphia Eagles, would eventually move to the top. This would also mean that league juggernauts like the Chicago Bears would not always be on top. This Halas didn't like, so nothing was done regarding a draft. Finally in 1936 Halas relented and backed the draft. He was always for "what's good for the league," if it eventually was good for the Chicago Bears. He came to the conclusion that in the long run, he could still get good players to keep the Bears on top.

Scouting was still primitive in those early years. Most teams relied on former players and fans to alert them about outstanding college talent. Also, newspaper accounts and football magazines provided teams with extra information about players. The Bears worked extremely hard at collecting data about potential draftees; they did their homework.

Prior to the first college draft, Halas made a trade with Philadelphia, exchanging two players he had planned to release for the rights to University of Chicago player Jay Berwanger. Berwanger was the top collegiate player and the winner of the first Heisman Trophy award, but he expressed little interest in playing professional football. Bert Bell, the Philadelphia owner, knew he had zero chance of signing Berwanger, so he was eager to trade the first pick. Halas, always the optimist, felt he could talk Berwanger into playing, so he made the deal— but it didn't happen. Berwanger stuck to his guns about not playing professional football and didn't sign with Chicago. Nonetheless, the Bears hit the jackpot in the first draft, getting two future Hall of Famers, Joe Stydahar and Danny Fortmann.

In 1939 Halas struck gold again. He traded star end Edgar "Eggs" Manske to Pittsburgh for the Steelers' top pick in the draft. That player turned out to be Columbia University quarterback Sid Luckman. As quarterback, Luckman would revolutionize the pro game. Luckman was a great passer, so Halas, with Clark Shaughnessy, brought the T formation to professional football to take advantage of Luckman's

Bronco Nagurski carries the football. © Brace Photo.

skills. With slight alterations to the offensive system Shaughnessy had run at Stanford, the T formation changed the pro game forever.

In 1940 the Bears had one of the great drafts in team history. First, Halas made a blockbuster trade with Philadelphia, getting All-American halfback George McAfee for a couple of no-name tackles. Besides getting future Hall of Fame center Clyde "Bulldog" Turner, the Bears drafted five other players that would go on to all-pro careers: Ken Kavanaugh and Hamp Pool, running back Harry Clark, and tackles Ed Kolman and Lee Artoe. George Halas always seemed to be one step ahead of the rest of the NFL.

The Bears would dominate the NFL in the 1940s, winning the title four times, with the last coming in 1946. During World War II Halas relinquished his coaching duties and entered the navy, returning to the Bears in 1946. In 1956–57 he stepped aside again while Bears legend John "Paddy" Driscoll coached the team. He was back at the helm by 1958, though, and he would remain there as the team entered the 1963 season.

WELLINGTON MARA (Owner, New York Giants): "One day in Wrigley Field an official ran to retrieve a punt that had gone out-of-bounds. He dropped his cap to mark the spot. George Halas moved it a foot or so in favor of the Bears. The distance meant absolutely nothing, but the action was typical of Halas. He just couldn't resist getting every possible advantage for the Bears. Of course the place was in an uproar. Another official finally moved the cap back. At the time, Halas's little act of enthusiasm didn't please me. I guess a person must become a little more mature, a little mellow, to appreciate the enthusiasm of someone who is always on the other side of the field."

MIKE DITKA (Tight End): "I was tremendously proud to put on a Bears uniform. I knew very little about the Bears until I was drafted by them in 1961, because I was from Pennsylvania and mostly followed the Pittsburgh Steelers and Philadelphia Eagles. But the more I found out about the Bears, the more I liked the team. Coach Halas taught the kind of football I believed in. The Bears were the Monsters of the Midway, the bullies, or whatever you want to call them. That was the way I thought the game of football was supposed to be played."

BILL WADE (Quarterback): "I would go down to the office with Coach Halas every Monday during the season, and look at the films of the previous game. We then would get some thoughts together about the game coming up. I really enjoyed that. It took a lot of time, but I enjoyed being with him. You know, it was like being with 'Mr. Football.' We would talk and usually go somewhere to have dinner before I would go home. He worked at least sixteen to eighteen hours every day. I admired him. I admired his tremendous work ethic."

ROGER DAVIS (Offensive Guard): "Before a road game we were going through the tunnel to the locker room and I was walking behind Coach Halas. I noticed that every once in a while he'd stop and put an X on the wall. Finally when we got to the locker room, I said, 'Coach, what are you doing with the Xs?' He said, 'I'm going to know how to get back to the bus when we leave here.' That was Coach Halas."

Chicago Bears Roster

No.	Name	Pos.	Ht.	Wt.	Age	Yrs. in NFL	School
9	Wade, Bill	QB	6'2	205	32	10	Vanderbilt
10	Bukich, Rudy	QB	6'2	205	31	9	So. Cal.
17	Petitbon, Richie	DB	6'3	205	25	5	Tulane
15	Keckin, Val	QB	6'3	218	25	1	Mississippi So.
20	Harmon, Dennis	DB	6'1	198	24	1	So. Illinois
21	Szumczyk, John	OHB	6'1	210	22	1	Trinity
22	Martin, Billy	HB	5'11	197	25	2	Minnesota
23	Whitsell, Dave	DB	6'1	190	27	6	Indiana
24	Taylor, Roosevelt	DB	5'11	186	26	3	Grambling
25	Caroline, J. C.	DB	6'1	190	30	8	Illinois
26	McRae, Bennie	DB	6'	180	22	2	Michigan
27	Banks, Gordon	DB	6'1	185	22	0	Fisk
28	Galimore, Willie	HB	6'1	187	28	7	Fla. A & M
29	Bull, Ronnie	HB	6'	200	23	2	Baylor
31	Fortunato, Joe	LB	6'1	225	32	9	Miss. St.
32	Powell, Preston	FB	6'2	225	26	2	Grambling
33	Morris, Larry	LB	6'2	230	28	8	Ga. Tech
34	Marconi, Joe	FB	6'2	225	29	8	West Virginia
35	Casares, Rick	FB	6'2	225	32	9	Florida
38	Moore, Woody	DB	6'	205	26	1	Indiana
41	Caylor, Lowell	DB	6'2	200	22	1	Miami (O.)
43	Glueck, Larry	DB	6'	190	21	1	Villanova
44	Gregory, John	DB	6'3	220	22	1	Baldwin Wallace
45	Yaksick, Bob	DB	6'2	200	22	1	Rutgers
46	Coie, Angelo	E	6'2	202	25	4	So. Cal.
47	Morris, Johnny	HB	5'10	180	28	6	U.C. Santa Barbara
48	Neck, Tommy	DB	5'11	190	24	2	Louisiana State
49	Bivins, Charles	HB	6'2	212	24	4	Morris Brown
50	Pyle, Mike	C	6'3	245	24	3	Yale
51	Vandersea, Howard	LB	6'4	225	21	1	Bates
52	Worrell, Bill	C	6'3	250	27	1	Hartnell
53	Von Sonn, Andy	LB	6'2	223	22	1	U.C.L.A.
54	Tyson, Randall	LB	6'2	225	22	1	Utah State
55	Coleman, Larry	OG	5'11	245	22	1	Indiana
58	Thomas, Ken	DT	6'5	292	23	1	Grambling
59	Jeralds, Luther	DE	6'3	238	25	1	N. Carolina St.
60	Davis, Roger	G	6'3	235	25	4	Syracuse
61	George, Bill	LB	6'2	235	32	12	Wake Forest
62	Bettis, Tom	LB	6'2	235	30	9	Purdue
63	Wetoska, Bob	T	6'3	240	26	4	Notre Dame
64	Marshall, Bobby	LB	6'	219	22	1	Virginia Union
65	Fanning, Stan	DT	6'7	270	25	4	Idaho
67	Karras, Ted	G	6'1	243	29	6	Indiana
68	Heerema,	OT	6'2	245	23	1	Central
69	Kenerson, John	DT	6'3	255	25	2	Kentucky State
70	Lee, Herman	T	6'3	247	30	6	Fla. A & M
71	Leggett, Earl	DT	6'3	250	30	7	La. St.
72	Cadile, Jim	OG	6'3	240	23	2	San Jose State
74	Kilcullen, Bob	DT	6'3	245	27	5	Texas Tech.
75	Williams, Fred	DT	6'4	248	33	12	Arkansas
73	Barnett, Steve	T	6'1	255	21	0	Oregon
78	Jones, Stan	G	6'1	250	31	10	Maryland
79	Anderson, Art	T	6'3	244	26	3	Idaho
80	Jencks, Bob	E	6'5	227	21	0	Miami (O.)
81	Atkins, Doug	DE	6'8	255	33	11	Tenn.
82	Youmans, Maury	DE	6'6	260	26	4	Syracuse
83	Leclerc, Roger	LB	235	235	26	4	Trinity
84	Farrington, John	E	6'3	217	27	4	Prairie View
85	Andrews, Dennis	OE	6'5	215	23	1	Virginia
86	Schulte, Eldon	LB	6'2	234	27	1	Central
87	O'Bradovich, Ed	DE	6'3	255	23	4	Illinois
88	Green, Bobby Joe	HB	5'11	175	27	2	Florida
89	Ditka, Mike	E	6'3	230	23	3	Pittsburgh

1963 preseason roster. Courtesy of Chicago Bears.

Wrigley Field. © Brace Photo.

Preseason

A NEW BEGINNING

Each year the College All-Star Game was played in Chicago in early August. *Chicago Tribune* sports editor Arch Ward came up with the idea in 1934 to benefit his newspaper's charity fund. Ward believed that an exhibition game between the reigning NFL champions and a team of college all-stars would make for a great game.

The first game ever played in this series proved to be very competitive as the all-stars and the Chicago Bears played to a scoreless tie. Through the first four years of the charity event, the college all-stars would hold their own, winning two of the games played. The all-stars' first win would come in 1937 when they defeated the Green Bay Packers 6–0. They would win again in 1938, beating the Washington Redskins 28–16. The games from that point on would be dominated by the NFL champions, who would win eighteen of the next twenty-four games played.

The 1963 game pitted the all-stars against the Green Bay Packers, who would be appearing in their second straight game. In 1962 the Packers had easily defeated the all-stars 42–20, and most football fans thought that the same thing would happen again. First, the Packers were that good and, second, a Vince Lombardi-coached team always played to win, exhibition game or not.

The all-stars, each year coached by Otto Graham, had three weeks to prepare for the game. In the past few years, Graham had scheduled a controlled scrimmage game against the Chicago Bears. He felt the experience would be good for his young players, giving them an idea of what to expect against pro competition. It would also give his coaching staff a chance to evaluate how the team was progressing.

George Halas used the scrimmage as one of the ways to make sure his players reported in good shape. Knowing the pride of professional athletes, Papa Bear always reminded the players during the off-season that they would be playing the college all-star team a few days after arriving at camp.

Unlike today, NFL players scattered to all parts of the country following the end of each football season. Most players went on to other jobs or careers to feed their families. NFL salaries were not substantial enough in the early 1960s to sustain players throughout the year. Each man was responsible for getting in shape on his own. There were no minicamps, no personal trainers, no football complexes to train at. When you arrived at camp, you had better be in shape and at your assigned weight. You had also better be ready to run the mile.

CHUCK MATHER (Coach): "I had encouraged George Halas to include the mile run for the players when they reported to camp to ensure that they were in shape. We set the time at seven minutes because I felt that if the Boy Scouts could run a mile under seven minutes to earn a merit badge, then a professional football player should also be able to do that. It was called the Halas Mile, and it served its purpose."

ROGER DAVIS (Offensive Guard): "I hated running that mile. Everybody did. You had to run it after practice after you were already tired from the first day's practice. The first couple of years I was unprepared to do that, but after that I was ready for it. If you were not prepared for it, it was a killer."

Each year Halas would assign players a certain weight to report to camp at. If a player was overweight, he was fined five dollars a pound for the first three pounds and twenty-five dollars a pound thereafter. The players were weighed once a week throughout the season.

BOB WETOSKA (Offensive Lineman): "I used to go and try to sweat my ass off and don't eat anything for twenty-four hours before the weigh-in. I was never clever enough to cheat on that. Guys had all kinds of different things that they would do, like sticking a ball of tape underneath the scale to rig it. One time they had a fishing line hung down from the ceiling that they would grab ahold of and pull themselves up to appear lighter than they actually were. Other guys would stand next to a guy and push his finger on the scale to make it read lighter. Finally the old man got wise to all that stuff, and he would push everybody away. You would then be by yourself with one of the assistant coaches watching you closely."

MIKE PYLE (Center): "Rick Casares had a foolproof method, according to Rick himself, of making weight. He would bypass food and drink martinis all evening. The next day he would be totally dehydrated and make his weight. He would barely make it through practice, but he would make his weight."

JOHNNY MORRIS (Flanker): "When I first came to the Bears there was the question whether I was big enough to play pro football. So when I weighed in I was always worried that I weighed enough. I had an assigned weight of 180 pounds, and sometimes to reach that weight I would put these rectangular two-pound weights under each of my arms. I would wear a T-shirt so the coaches couldn't detect the weights."

Each day the morning practices would start at 9:00 A.M. sharp. If you were late, you were fined five dollars per minute. Doug Atkins, never fond of practice, sometimes had a different routine.

ED O'BRADOVICH (Defensive End): "The first day of training camp Halas gives his speech, but Doug Atkins is not there. Halas finishes his talk, and we break up into our groups and begin doing our defensive drills. Still there's no Doug. Finally out comes Doug in some blue shorts, no T-shirt, a helmet without a face mask, and a white chin guard. He ran right by us down this road which was lined with Christmas trees. Then he ran all the way down the length of the field, way down to this back road. He only stopped and walked a couple of times. He comes all the way back, and when he came back Halas was sitting in his golf cart watching him. He never took his eyes off of him as he ran. It must have taken Doug about twenty minutes, and we were all watching him—everybody was watching him. We were practicing, and Doug runs right by the old man. The old man's neck is twisted around, but Doug does not say one word to him. When we finished practice and had taken a shower, we had to go to this meeting, but still no Doug. After the meeting we went to the line for lunch, and there Doug was— he was in the line for lunch. I said, 'Doug, what the hell are you doing? You ran around the field, you never said anything to anybody, you ran right by the old man, and you ran inside. What the hell were you doing?' He said, 'I was breaking in my new helmet.' That was his answer for missing practice, missing the meeting . . . he was breaking in his helmet."

STAN JONES (Defensive Tackle): "At training camp Rick Casares had a little dog. I think it was a terrier. That dog took a crap every day right outside Halas's room at the dormitory. I think Rick trained it to take a crap right outside of Halas's door."

On a hot day in late July, the college all-star team bused up to Rensselaer, Indiana, to scrimmage the Bears. Chicago, in camp only a few days, never brought their "A game" to these contests, but nonetheless through personal pride and George Halas's prodding they always played with emotion.

MIKE DITKA (Tight End): "In 1961 I was with the college all-stars when we scrimmaged the Bears. I did not make any friends on that day as I ran over a couple of guys. Those scrimmages were always hard played."

The all-stars, fired up for their first pro experience, played hard throughout the scrimmage, giving the Bears all they could handle before losing 13–12 on a blocked extra point. The all-stars' defense, led by Bobby Bell and Jim Dunaway, played solidly throughout the scrimmage, limiting the Bears to only two touchdowns.

Chicago scored first when halfback Charlie Bivins ran in from five yards out. Mike Ditka, seemingly stopped at the 5-yard line, lateraled to a surprised Bivins who sprinted in for the score. Roger LeClerc's extra point was wide. The second touchdown again involved Mike Ditka as he caught a short pass from Bill Wade and rambled 16 yards for the score, bowling over two defenders on his way to the goal line. LeClerc's kick this time was good.

The all-stars' first points of the scrimmage came on two field goals by 1963 Bears draftee Bob Jencks. Their only touchdown came late in the scrimmage on a nifty 14-yard run by Charlie Mitchell. The speedy halfback ran left, then sprinted back across the grain into the end zone, cutting the Bears' lead to one point. The extra-point attempt was blocked by crafty veteran J. C. Caroline who sped in untouched to bat the attempt away, preserving the Bears' win.

Overall George Halas was pleased with the scrimmage. No injuries had occurred, and he had substituted freely, taking a long look at his rookie players. At times his defense looked strong, so it was a good beginning to training camp. Offensively, they needed more work perfecting the new plays, but both Wade and Rudy Bukich had looked in control. The all-stars had played well against the Bears and were brimming with confidence traveling back to Chicago. A week later they would stun the Green Bay Packers, upsetting them 20–17.

George Halas always looked forward to training camp. It was a time of year that the old coach could totally focus on coaching his team. Being the only head-coach/owner in the NFL would at times pull him in different directions. Being organized and able to delegate responsibility had made him a legend in the game. These few weeks in Rensselaer were all about coaching football. "Nothing is work unless you'd rather be doing something else," he would tell his players. Coaching football was his passion, his love. And he approached it with vigor. It was the happiest part of the year, preparing his team for another season.

GEORGE HALAS (Owner/Head Coach, Chicago Bears): "Football practice is monotonous and tiring. Sometimes it becomes extremely fatiguing. However, it is all part of the game. Drill . . . drill . . . and still more drills are necessary to perfect the fundamentals. The mental satisfaction of winning a championship far outweighs any momentary discomfort. When you leave the field physically fatigued but feeling mentally refreshed, you are on the right track."

The Bears, following the all-star scrimmage, settled down to practicing twice a day and preparing for their first exhibition game against the New York Giants. Having lost to Green Bay the past two years in the championship game had left the Giants hungry to get back a third time and win. Led by quarterback Y. A. Tittle, the Giants were one of the NFL's most dominant teams in the early 1960s, averaging 28 points a game in 1962. Easily winning the Eastern Conference with a 12–2 record last season, this veteran-dominated team would again be the front runner to return to the championship game. Middle linebacker Sam Huff and defensive end Andy Robustelli were the leaders on a very solid Giants defensive team.

Allie Sherman, in his third year as the Giants' head coach, had posted an impressive 22–5–1 record. Replacing incumbent coach Jim Lee Howell in 1961, Sherman had won back-to-back Coach of the Year Awards.

The youthful coach's ties to the New York team went back to the late 1940s when as an assistant to head coach Steve Owen he had been instrumental in transforming Charlie Connerly into a competent T-formation quarterback. After a stint with the Canadian League, Sherman returned to the Giants in 1957 as a full-time scout. In his promotion to the head coaching position in 1961, Sherman had demonstrated an ability to add key players to the roster. Working closely with Giants owner Wellington Mara, one of Sherman's first moves was to pry the veteran Tittle away from the San Francisco 49ers. Concerned that the aging Connerly couldn't hold up under a fourteen-game schedule, the Giants traded for Tittle. The initial plan was to use him as a backup to Connerly, but the Giants found out quickly that Tittle still had some good football in him. In 1961 he won the starting job by completely outplaying Connerly during the exhibition season. He was the main reason the Giants had been in the championship game the past two years. This Giants game would be a good test for the Bears.

The Giants had beaten the Bears 26–24 last year in a hard-hitting game that was marred by many fights. The main event that day was between Ed O'Bradovich and Giants halfback Phil King, who took exception to O'Bradovich's late hit. Unfortunately, because of a throat infection, O'Bradovich would not be available for the rematch, but players on both sides were approaching the game with emotion.

Early in the second quarter former Bears defensive back Erich Barnes tackled Bill Wade out-of-bounds. Bears guard Roger Davis took exception to the play and punched Barnes in the mouth. Players erupted from both sides, with order finally being restored after ten

Halas and Lombardi. Courtesy of Ron Nelson/Prairie Street Art.

minutes of chaos. Later in the game tempers flared again as Mike Ditka teed off on Giants defensive back Tom Scott. Ditka felt Scott was getting away with holding him and threw the Giants defender to the ground. The Bears' Ted Karras, seeing Ditka's displeasure, squared off against Giants defensive end Andy Robustelli. Rookie Bob Jencks, not to be outdone, drew the ire of Giants defensive back Dick Lynch as both got into a pushing match. When the game finally ended the Bears prevailed 17–7. Held to only three points in the first half, the Bears rallied for two touchdowns behind the fine quarterback play of Rudy Bukich. First, Bukich hit split end John Farrington for 12 yards and a touchdown in the third quarter, then Bukich came back to Farrington in the fourth quarter, this time on a beautiful 37-yard pass. Farrington split to the left side, faked an inside move, then sprinted past Giants defensive back Jimmy Patton for the score.

The Bears' offense garnered twenty-one first downs on 192 yards rushing and 181 yards passing. Rick Casares and Ronnie Bull did the lion's share of carrying the ball, but three fumbles—two recovered by the Giants—tarnished a good overall offensive performance. On defense the Bears were solid against the run, allowing only 40 yards rushing, but gave up more than 200 yards passing.

Both coaches shook hands after the game, and as each turned to leave Allie Sherman grabbed Halas's elbow. "George, I hope we meet at the end of the year when it counts." George Halas, nodding his head, smiled and walked away.

BILL WADE (Quarterback): "I thought in training camp in '63 that we had the capability of being a championship team. All the talk that year about the defense this, the defense that, but if you look at the scores of some of the games you'll see that the offense did its job. I never said anything publicly because to me a team is a team. When you start saying defense this, offensive that, you're making a big mistake. All you're doing is separating the team. I'd been through that with the Rams, and any time somebody starts trying to put in thoughts that would separate the team, to me all they were doing was hurting the team. I never tried to add any fuel to that type of attitude."

On their return to camp the Bears prepared for their next game, against the Washington Redskins. Washington began the 1962 season 4–0–2 but lost seven of the last eight games to finish 5–7–2. Coach Bill McPeak felt the first half of the 1962 season was more indicative of his team's play versus the second half when injuries had taken their toll. Sticking with quarterback Norm Snead, McPeak felt his team could challenge the Giants and Browns in the Eastern Conference. In wide receiver Bobby Mitchell, quarterback Norm Snead had an excellent target to throw to. The elusive Mitchell, since being converted from a running back to a wide receiver, had become a big-time player, catching eleven touchdown passes in 1962. Running back Billy Barnes was the workhorse in the backfield, gaining 492 yards on 159 carries last season. Don Bossler, Jim Cunningham, Leroy Jackson, and Dick James rounded out the backfield.

The exhibition game played in Washington turned out to be an impressive offensive showing by both teams, with the Bears holding on to win 28–26. Chicago came out in the first quarter with their offense clicking and moved down the field twice with sustained scoring drives. Quarterback Bill Wade and fullback Rick Casares both scored on short runs to give the visitors a 14–0 first-quarter lead. Washington, sparked by quarterback Norm Snead's outstanding passing, stormed back in the second quarter, scoring 23 unanswered points to take a 23–14 lead at the half. In the third quarter, Chicago's Billy Martin gave the momentum back to his team. Fielding a punt on his own 23-yard line, Martin sidestepped a tackler at the 25-yard line, then burst up the middle, cut hard to his right, picked up a block from Mike Ditka, and sprinted 77 yards for the touchdown, cutting Washington's lead to 23–21. In the fourth quarter the Bears struck again. Rudy Bukich, from his 32-yard line, found John Farrington wide open on a crossing pattern. Farrington, catching the ball in stride, outran two Washington defenders to the goal line. The play, good for 68 yards, put the Bears in front 28–23.

Not to be outdone, Washington marched back down the field, settling on a 14-yard Bob Khayat field goal to cut the Bears' lead to 28–26. Late in the game, backup quarterback George Izo moved the Redskins again into position to win the game. Khayat's 32-yard kick sailed wide as the gun sounded. The Bears had escaped 28–26.

The Bears' defense, supposedly the backbone of the team, had played poorly, allowing the Redskins to move the ball at will. On offense the Bears continued to improve. Bill Wade in the first half had directed the team on two long scoring drives, and his replacement, Rudy Bukich, also performed well. There seemed to be no drop-off in production when either player was in the game.

John Farrington was becoming an imposing target for the quarterbacks. The lanky end with blazing speed was becoming a reliable target, catching everything thrown his way. He was becoming the key receiver in the Bears' offense.

Coach Halas was pleased with the direction the offense was going but disgusted with his defense's inconsistent performances. Two weeks in a row teams had moved the ball well through the air. The pass defense needed to improve, as this type of effort would not be acceptable in the regular season. The Bears would be lucky to win any games when the defense played like that. That had to change.

One Bear player wasn't so lucky. Maury Youmans injured his knee in the second quarter. At first thought a leg bruise, the injury was much more serious: there was cartilage damage.

MAURY YOUMANS (Defensive End): "I remember it was a passing situation, and I tried to make a move to the inside when I heard my knee pop. It locked right up on me, and I could not bend it. I just hopped off the field. The next day they sent me to Chicago where Dr. Fox operated on it. He told me afterwards that I had stretched the cartilage and ligament so much that he could wrap them around my knee like a tie. I was supposed to be out six weeks, but the knee became infected, which cost me the season."

Injuries, so much a part of the game, can quickly turn a promising year into despair in the National Football League. All coaches walk the fine line in training camp on how much time to play their regulars in preparing them for the regular season. George Halas was no exception. The loss of Youmans for the year and Ed O'Bradovich still not able to play left the Bears with only one healthy, experienced defensive end: Doug Atkins. Adding to the team's list of health problems, Mike Ditka had missed most of the Washington game with a leg pull. Flanker Johnny Morris was still struggling with a leg injury, and running back Willie Galimore had yet to see any contact. Halas decided to move linebacker Roger LeClerc and tackle Bob Kilcullen to the outside on defense. Playing the Packers was tough enough, but with a depleted squad it would be a huge challenge. Nonetheless, it was the Green Bay Packers—who couldn't get excited about that?

BOB WETOSKA (Offensive Lineman): "I remember in training camp our first meeting with Halas. He said we were going to dedicate this training camp to beating the Green Bay Packers the opening game. He said that every practice in Rensselaer will include at least fifteen minutes of practicing against the Packers' offense. Every day we did that,

Maury Youmans. © 1963 by Laughead Photographers, courtesy of Chicago Bears.

building through all the exhibition season to beat the Green Bay Packers that first game. Psychologically he was preparing us to do that."

Vince Lombardi, following his team being upset by the college all-stars, had been cracking the whip. The Packers, embarrassed over the defeat, had taken apart the Pittsburgh Steelers 27–7 and the Dallas Cowboys 31–10 the past two weeks. Dealing with the loss of Paul Hornung, who with Detroit's Alex Karras had been suspended for the entire season for gambling, the Packers' offense was beginning to play well. Running backs Tom Moore and Elijah Pitts were being called upon to pick up the slack in Hornung's absence. At fullback, Jim Taylor was healthy and ready to go.

The NFL regular season now just a few weeks away, both coaches decided to play it close to the vest for this exhibition game. Each team, not giving away any new plays, just lined up and whacked each other hard for sixty minutes.

Chicago drew first blood in the game on a short Wade-to-Ditka touchdown pass. Midway through the second quarter, trailing 7–0, the Packers drove to the Bears' 19-yard line. Faking a dive play to Taylor, Bart Starr dropped back and floated a perfect spiral to tight end Ron Kramer for the touchdown. J. C. Caroline, lining up on the right side, blocked the extra point to keep the Bears in front 7–6 at halftime.

The Packers' offense, which looked sluggish in the first half, came out firing on all cylinders to start the third quarter. Returning the kickoff to the Bears' 30-yard line, the Packers marched straight down the field where Bart Starr found old pro Max McGee over the middle for the touchdown. This time Jerry Kramer's extra point was good.

With Rudy Bukich now at quarterback, the Bears moved back down the field on a series of short passes and the strong running of Ronnie Bull. Reaching the Packer 1-yard line, the Bears were unable to score on three Rick Casares dives. Facing a fourth-down decision, Halas went for the touchdown, but Ronnie Bull's attempt fell 3 inches short of pay dirt. The Packers had held.

Early in the fourth quarter tempers flared, and the Packers' star receiver Boyd Dowler was ejected from the game. The Packers' offense continued to move the ball well against the Bears' defense, pushing deep into Chicago territory where Kramer kicked a 27-yard field goal to extend the lead to 16–7.

At this point both coaches gave their rookies and second-line players a chance to play, pulling their starting players from the game. Green Bay would put ten more points on the board, which included a 27-yard touchdown by linebacker Dave Robinson off an errant Bukich pass. The final score had Green Bay winning 26–7.

Following the game Halas lamented about the 88-yard drive in the third quarter that came up 3 inches short of a touchdown. "There is no doubt in my mind that Rick Casares scored on third down," Halas said. "There was an official standing there who saw the whole thing, but they took it away from us," the old coach added.

BILL WADE (Quarterback): "I also thought Casares scored. I fully believe Rick Casares scored in the third period. I can't prove it and neither can Casares. Why can't a photographic device be installed on both goal lines of football fields to take a picture of a close play, just as the camera records a dead heat at Arlington Park?"

Halas was pleased with his team's ability to move the ball against the Packers. Offensive-line coach Phil Handler was doing a great job, and rookie tackle Steve Barnett was catching everyone's eye with his outstanding play. The Bears had made a huge gamble by permanently moving the great Stan Jones to defense this year. The young rookie was filling the void at tackle very nicely.

STAN JONES (Defensive Tackle): "In 1962 I went from playing offense to playing defense. Halas caught me before a meeting started and said, 'Stan, this week you are going to have to play defense. Run over to the defensive meeting room.' I go over there and they all shut up, as Shaughnessy thought I was a spy. I thought, my God, I don't know the defenses. I'm playing the game and I don't really know the defense. George Allen told me to sit with him on the airplane. He sat with me on the airplane and gave me some cards he was writing up on the different defenses. If it wasn't for that, I would not have known what the hell I was doing."

Halfback Willie Galimore was finally given full clearance to play. The veteran back was anxious to test his surgically repaired knees in game competition, and his longtime head coach was also anxious to see him play. "We wanted Willie to have plenty of opportunity to round into shape slowly," Halas said. "He has been cutting well in the past few practices and we feel he's ready for his first big test." Galimore's presence would reduce the workload of Ronnie Bull. Bull had gained 70 yards against the Packers, giving the second-year pro 180 yards rushing on just 40 carries thus far in the exhibition season. It was time to cut him back and take a look at Galimore and Charlie Bivins.

Defensive-line coach Joe Stydahar, unhappy with his defensive linemen's play, was going back to the basics and focusing on defensive techniques. "We're paying more attention to the little details this week," explained Stydahar. "We're concentrating on the use of the forearm and the movement of the head. We're just trying to go back to some old fashion Bears football."

The players had been in camp for four weeks and were looking forward to getting the exhibition season over with. This week they would be playing the Armed Forces Game at Soldier Field against the St. Louis Cardinals.

Practices were reduced to one a day but were very physical. The coaching staff was cracking down hard on mistakes, and the roster was getting smaller and smaller each week. Veterans and rookies were feeling the pressure to win a roster spot. Every player knew that if you were cut this late in the preseason, it would be next to impossible to catch on with another team. Every day was all-out war.

The St. Louis Cardinals had left Chicago for St. Louis three years before, in 1960. Originally starting out as a neighborhood team in the rough Irish section of Chicago in 1899, the team was known as the Morgan Athletic Club. Later when the team was playing its home games at Chicago's Normal Field, they became the Chicago Normals. A few years later owner Chris O'Brien bought some used jerseys at a great price from the University of Chicago. The crimson color reminded O'Brien of the ill-tempered bird, and the team's nickname became the Cardinals.

The team struggled in those early years, always playing second fiddle to the Bears. Led by Paddy Driscoll, they would win the championship in 1925, but due to financial troubles O'Brien was forced to sell Driscoll to the Bears a year later. In 1947 the Cardinals, now under the ownership of the Charles Bidwell family, would win the championship again. Mostly a second-division team, the Cardinals finally received a financial proposal from the city of St. Louis that was too good to turn down and moved west.

The Cardinals' won-lost record in 1962 was 4–9–1, but with star running back John David Crow healthy and the continued development of quarterback Charlie Johnson, the Cards were optimistic going into the 1963 season. Coach Wally Lemm felt that his team had the best depth at running back in the Eastern Conference with Crow,

Prentis Gault, Joe Childress, Bill Triplett, and rookie Bill "Thunder" Thornton. Up front the offensive line was very good, led by tackle Ernie McMillan and center Bob DeMarco. On defense they had become stronger with the addition of rookie linebacker Larry Stallings who was making a huge impact this exhibition season. There was cause for much optimism in St. Louis this year.

A crowd of 60,884 turned out to watch the Bears and Cardinals clash for the seventy-sixth time. After a scoreless first period, the Bears' offense began to roll behind the superb play calling of Bill Wade. Marching to the Cardinal 6-yard line, Ronnie Bull slashed off tackle for the game's first score. The Bears added to their lead early in the third quarter when Wade spotted Johnny Morris behind the Cardinal secondary. Stepping up in the pocket to avoid the outside rush, Wade heaved a long pass downfield that Morris ran under at the 5-yard line for a spectacular 61-yard touchdown.

St. Louis, now behind in the game 14–0, started their comeback from their own 20-yard line. Quarterback Charlie Johnson moved his offense straight down the field with precision. Johnson, aware of playing against Chicago's reserve players, exploited the Bears' inexperienced secondary on each play. The Cardinals reached the Bears' 5-yard line where Johnson connected with a wide-open Billy Gambrell in the back of the end zone for the touchdown.

Midway through the fourth quarter St. Louis again moved into the Bears' territory but had to settle for a Jim Bakken 28-yard field goal.

Now trailing 14–10, the Cardinals needed to put together one more drive to finish the comeback and win the game. Charlie Johnson, facing a strong Chicago rush, was forced out of the pocket. Sprinting to his right, the Cardinals' quarterback completed a pass to Gambrell who motored down to the Bears' 24-yard line. On the next play he faked a handoff to Crow, then hit veteran wide receiver Sonny Randle at the goal line for the winning score. The Cardinals had rallied for a 17–14 victory.

George Halas was subdued following the loss. He had rested his regulars for most of the second half, which is when the Cardinals had the most success moving the ball. Although the Bears had one more exhibition game, against the Baltimore Colts, the old coach was already thinking ahead to the Packer game in two weeks. That was what all this hard work was all about.

ED O'BRADOVICH (Defensive End): "I played next to Freddy Williams on the defensive line. Every year we would play the old Armed Forces Game at Soldier Field. Freddy was chosen one year as the MVP in one game. He said, 'Ed, I really didn't deserve it. I really didn't deserve it, but that is just my humble opinion against sixty thousand other people's opinions.' "

While the Bears were preparing for their last exhibition game, in New Orleans, word had come out that Philadelphia Eagles quarterback Sonny Jurgensen and his backup, King Hill, had walked out of training camp over contract disputes. Jurgensen, unsigned for 1963, was seeking a contract of thirty thousand dollars, an increase of five thousand dollars over last year. Hill was upset over the Eagles offering him less than the reported twenty thousand dollars he made in 1962. Frustrated with the Eagles' failure to negotiate, both players walked out.

In 1963 all NFL contracts contained an option clause that bound the players to their respective teams for one year. This clause severely limited the players' negotiating abilities. Players could become a free agent by either sitting out a year or play out the option under last year's terms. Jurgensen and King decided to protest this unfair option clause by walking out. Adding to the Eagles' woes was that four other players in camp were unsigned. Eventually, the matter was resolved, but the two players had taken a unified stance regarding the unfairness of the option clause. It caught the attention of all the NFL players.

After two straight losses, the Bears were looking to rebound with a good performance in the Big Easy. Their game against the Colts would be part of an NFL doubleheader. First, the Detroit Lions would take on the Dallas Cowboys, followed by the Colts and Bears' contest thirty minutes later. The games would be played at the Sugar Bowl with an expected crowd of more than seventy thousand fans. The game was being promoted by the city of New Orleans, which in 1963 was attempting to establish itself as a major sports center. The city's hope was to eventually lure an NFL franchise to the area.

The Colts, under new head coach Don Shula, were looking to rebound from a 7–7 season. The thirty-three-year-old Shula was being given his first chance to be a head coach in the NFL, replacing long-time coach Weeb Ewbank. Last year the Colts had been up and down, playing well at times but overall inconsistently. Starting to show some age, many players were still on the roster from the glory years of the late 1950s. Quarterback Johnny Unitas threw for twenty-three touchdowns last year, mainly to receivers Jimmy Orr and Raymond Berry, who caught fifty-five and fifty-one passes, respectively. Halfbacks Lenny Moore and Tom Matte and fullback Joe Perry completed the backfield, with multipurpose player Alex Hawkins providing depth off the bench. Gino Marchetti, Ordelle Brasse, Bobby Boyd, and Lenny Lyles led an aging defense. In 1962 the Bears had beaten the Colts twice, 35–15 at Wrigley Field then crushing them at Memorial Stadium 57–0. Baltimore, looking for a new direction, had turned to Shula. Undefeated in their first four exhibition games, the Colts were playing with much more enthusiasm and were once again looking to be a factor in the Western Conference.

The NFL doubleheader, on a hot, steamy night in New Orleans, opened with the Dallas Cowboys looking sharp in defeating the Detroit Lions 27–17. Late in that contest, heavy rains came as a storm blew into the bayou. Unfortunately for the teams and the seventy thousand fans in attendance, the rain did not stop. The torrential downpour flooded the field, causing the second contest to start an hour late. When it was all over, the Bears had slopped to a 14–7 win. Given the conditions, both coaches held back key players, as the field was a sea of mud and water. All the yard markers were washed away, and visibility was limited.

The Colts' offense, under the direction of veteran Lamar McHan and rookie Gary Cuozzo, never was able to mount much of an attack. The Bears' offense also struggled but did score a touchdown to open the game, aided by three Baltimore penalties.

Both sides were glad when this exhibition game came to a merciful end. Unfortunately, the Bears lost two more players to injury. Billy Martin, who had shown signs of brilliance as a punt returner, had broken his fibula and would be sidelined indefinitely. Tom Bettis, subbing for Larry Morris at outside linebacker, reinjured his elbow. His status for next week's opener against the Packers was doubtful.

Stan Jones. Courtesy of Chicago Bears.

Halas was happy to have the preseason over. His team had gone
3–2 in the exhibition games. At times Halas saw glimpses of greatness,
but the team still lacked consistency. Some of the poor play was due to
rookies and second-line players, but he worried that they still were not
at the level he thought they should be. He was glad it was time to play
for keeps. One big hurdle lay ahead: in seven days the Bears would be
taking on the world champions. Halas vowed to have his team ready.

STAN JONES (Defensive Tackle): "One time we asked for Sundays off from practice during the preseason because we would get back
so late from the exhibition games. Guys didn't want to have to go out
on the field on Sunday. So everybody was on my ass about it and say-

ing, 'Hey, Stan, ask him if we can have Sundays off.' So I said at a meeting one day, 'Coach, why is it we are the only team in the NFL that practices on Sunday after a Saturday game? Why is it we are the only team that does not have Sundays off?' He said, 'Simply because we practice on Sunday, Stan.'

"After the meeting one of the players said, 'Stan, he is quite religious. Why don't you tell him the Protestant boys can't go to church on Sunday because we are all out there on the practice field during church?' I went over there and I talked to him. I said, 'Coach, the Protestant boys would like to go to church on Sunday morning.' He said, 'How many would be interested in going?' I said, 'Well, you figure about half the boys that are Protestant.' He said, 'Well, if you can promise me that they all go, if they all go or a good portion of them go, you can have Sunday mornings off.' Boy, what a religious revival that was. . . . We filled that Methodist church in Rensselaer. We got everybody out of bed and pushed people down there. We got them all down to the First Methodist Church in Rensselaer."

MAURY YOUMANS (Defensive End): "It was the end of training camp and Halas was giving us a talk a week before the first game. He says, 'You know, we are in Chicago now, so it is going to be a lot different from training camp. I want you guys to get rid of that dreaded disease before Thursday, Penis Erecta, because I want you guys ready to play.' "

Doug Atkins. Courtesy of Doug Atkins.

Two Monsters of the Midway

DOUG ATKINS AND BILL GEORGE

Doug Atkins

In October 1960 the Baltimore Colts were playing the Chicago Bears in Chicago. Colts quarterback Johnny Unitas dropped back to pass, and to avoid being sacked by Bears linebacker Bill George he moved out of the pocket. He glanced to his right and saw number 81 bearing down on him. Having been sacked by this monster of a man before, Unitas tried to fall down to reduce the force of this inevitable contact, but he reacted too late. Doug Atkins hit him with such fury that the quarterback later said he could feel his whole body shake.

The Baltimore quarterback being slammed to the ground felt his single-bar face mask smash against his nose, instantly breaking it. Lying on the ground bleeding, with his whole body in pain, Unitas could hear Atkins talking to him. "Stay down, John, or I'm going to have to give you some more."

Doug Atkins grew up in rural Tennessee during the depression. His family, like most families during that period in American history, struggled to make ends meet. His father, a painter and carpenter by trade, would accept any work available to earn money for his family. Unfortunately, his thirst for liquor often saw his daily earnings drunk away. The entire family would pitch in during these tough times to see that there was food on the table and a roof over their heads. When Doug was twelve, he went to work packing tomatoes.

DOUG ATKINS (Defensive End): "We were poor but we didn't know we were poor. My daddy worked a while, then drank a while. He got in the fruit business. Back in those days they packed tomatoes in twenty-pound crates. Before the season we would make those crates, and I got so I was pretty good at putting them together. Then during the season I would go around after they were loaded and nail them up. Then we would load them on the boxcars. It was very tough work, but I was making fifty dollars a week, which was pretty good money for a twelve-year-old boy."

Atkins in his freshmen year in high school decided to go out for the football team. Weighing only 118 pounds, he was no match for the bigger boys, but he impressed the coach with his strong determination. By the time he reached his senior year he stood 6'8", and was 195 pounds of muscle. This mountain of a man, besides being an outstanding football player, excelled in basketball and high-jumped 6'6" in the state track meet. His prowess won him a full scholarship to the University of Tennessee. Recruited for football, Doug decided he wanted to concentrate on basketball, but Tennessee football coach General Robert Neyland was not a man to take no for an answer. He quickly changed that attitude in his young player.

DOUG ATKINS (Defensive End): "General Neyland made it clear that I was there to play football. I could play other sports, but I was definitely going to play football. He was the most organized coach you would ever see. We would be in practice, and he would know everything that was going on. If you weren't doing what you should be doing, he'd hightail it over to you and give you hell. He was an old army man who had graduated from West Point.

Big Doug back home in Tennessee. Courtesy of Doug Atkins.

"My brother was there the year he got to Tennessee. He said they'd had some tough boys on the team at that time—they were renegades, they were rough. When Neyland first got there, these boys were making fun of him, kind of feeling him out. He wore at that time his army uniform to practice. One day he told them, 'Boys, I'll tell you what. Why don't you pick out your toughest, meanest guy, and I'll put the boxing gloves on with him.' He always had a pair of boxing gloves at practice. If anybody had a fight during our practices, they would take their helmets off and put those gloves on quick-like, while they were still mad. They just would go at it. He'd make them fight till they dropped. Pretty soon there wasn't any fights at practice, because even if you won them, you lost. Anyway, the next day they picked the guy they wanted to fight Neyland. This ol' boy was a big, rough-looking guy. My brother said he thought, if this ol' boy hits Neyland, we won't have a football team. They put the gloves on, and Neyland would dance around, throw a jab, then a punch, then bounce back. He said when Neyland would hit that boy, he would twist his glove. In a short time he had that ol' boy bleeding like a stuck hog. That boy would take a swing at him, but Neyland would step aside. Finally that ol' boy said he'd had enough. From that day on Neyland had those boys' attention. It turned out Neyland was the heavyweight boxing champion at West Point."

Doug Atkins settled into college life and with three square meals a day began to fill out his 6'8" frame. A three-year starter on the Volunteer football team, he was chosen to the All-America team his senior year. The Cleveland Browns made him their first pick in the 1953 draft.

DOUG ATKINS (Defensive End): "I didn't know I was drafted. After we lost in the Cotton Bowl my senior year, I was tired of school. I met this guy at a local beer joint. He had been touring the country playing basketball with this team called the Detroit Vagabonds. We're sitting there drinking beer, and I asked him, did he need someone else to play? He said, 'You know, we just lost a guy who got married, but you want to go to school and get an education.' I said, 'No!' That's the last thing I wanted to do. 'I'm ready to get out of here. How much do you pay?' He said he would call me in the morning because he first had to talk to the owner of the team. He called me in the morning and said, 'It's all set.' I said, 'Well, how much do you pay?' He said, '$350 a month plus expenses.' Goodness, that was like a gold mine to me. Later I'm walking out of the dorm with this old cardboard suitcase, and I meet one of the Tennessee coaches. He said, 'Doug, where you going?' I said, 'I'm getting the hell out of here.' He said, 'Can't we talk about it?' He wanted me to go out for track. I said, 'No, I'm gone.' That was the happiest day of my life. I hated school as I had been playing football and basketball and track year-round. I had no time to do anything else.

"We took off the next day in a 1952 Ford Coupe. They also had this big old Chrysler limousine. I had a good time with that team traveling all over the country. I had three great months. One day the coach said that Weeb Ewbank of the Cleveland Browns was coming to see me as he wanted to sign me to play football with the Cleveland Browns. Weeb shows up and he and I went to this joint, where he bought me a cheeseburger. I was drinking a beer listening to him. He was talking football, and he offered me $6,500. I think at that time I had drank about seven or eight beers. I finally got him up to, I think, $6,800 dollars. He made like he had to go make a call to get Paul Brown's okay. I signed the contract right there for $6,800, two cheeseburgers, and eight beers. Today they get a $5 million signing bonus. Afterwards Weeb told me Paul Brown said he could have gone up to $8,500. I said, 'Why, you little prick, I ought to wring your neck!' That's a true story."

The first year in Cleveland Atkins made an immediate impact on the Browns' defense, helping the team win the divisional title in 1953 and the NFL Championship the following year. Never shy about expressing his opinion, Atkins quarreled with Paul Brown repeatedly. Brown's style of coaching didn't sit well with the big defensive end.

DOUG ATKINS (Defensive End): "Paul Brown was a smart man, and he knew his football. He would make us take tests, and I hated tests. That's why I got out of school—because of those tests. Not only did we have to learn our own position on every play, we had to learn everyone else's as well. Heck, I had to cheat like hell to get through those tests. That's the only thing I worried about when I was with the Browns, taking those damned tests."

In his second year, during training camp, Doug injured his knee and also developed an ulcer. When his defensive play slipped because of injuries, Paul Brown threatened to release him. Coach and player were growing apart.

DOUG ATKINS (Defensive End): "I got an ulcer my second year and lost thirty pounds. Also, my knee was acting up. He calls me in and says he's not sure I can make the team. He heard I had been out 'tomcatting' around, not concentrating on football. He was all over me. We had this diner where we would all go to eat after practice. There was a song out, 'Rub-a-Dub-Dub, Three Men in a Tub,' that was popular at that time. Someone told me Paul Brown hated that song. So one day at the diner I decided to play that song. I played it over and over, 'Rub-a-Dub-Dub, Three Men in a Tub.' It drove him crazy."

To no one's surprise, Atkins was traded to the Chicago Bears after the second season. At Chicago he began to show glimpses of becoming a great player. A rare combination of strength, size, and speed, he could turn an offensive lineman's Sunday into a nightmare. You didn't want to get him mad.

JIM PARKER (Offensive Guard): "I played against some mean players in my time with Baltimore, but I never played against anyone meaner than Doug Atkins. After my first meeting with him, I really wanted to quit pro ball."

ROGER DAVIS (Offensive Guard): "Before my first team scrimmage with the Bears, the veterans told me to be sure not to go low and make him mad. I had heard stories about him beating up players who did that. I can assure you I never went low or made him mad."

Atkins won the Most Valuable Lineman Award in the 1959 Pro Bowl and earned All-NFL honors in 1960 and 1961. Halas saw greatness in Atkins but wished he would play with more anger. These two strong-willed men worked well together, but their personal battles became legendary.

DOUG ATKINS (Defensive End): "I got along okay with Halas until he started ragging me about playing better. We had this meeting and he says, 'Doug, why don't you play football like the Colts' defensive end Gino Marchetti?' I said, 'Coach, why don't you lend me $50,000 like [Baltimore Colts owner] Rosenblum did him?' I said, 'I might just show you Marchetti or maybe a little more. Lend me that $50,000 like Rosenblum, put me in a four-man rush, and turn me loose instead of all these loop-de-loop defenses. I just might show you Marchetti, and maybe I might show you a little more.' That set him off real good."

BILL WADE (Quarterback): "Coach Halas tried to deal with people on an individual basis. He and Doug Atkins would go at it. It was like 'organized dissension' between the two of them. I was living in the room next to Halas in training camp. Many times I heard he and Doug talking, and I can tell you they weren't praising each other.

"I remember when Coach Halas decided he was going to find the person that was stealing money at Halas Hall during training camp. He said, 'I'm going to find out who is stealing the money.' So he got a flashlight, and he started going into the rooms one by one. Doug saw him coming and hid behind the door. He got a blanket, and when Coach Halas came into his room with a flashlight, Doug put the blanket over his head, lifted him up, carried him out into the hall, and said, 'I caught the thief, I caught the thief!' Halas is squirming in Doug's blanket. Everyone comes out into the hall, and Doug's yelling, 'I got the thief.' You could hear Halas under the blanket saying, 'Doug, this is George Halas. Now let me down.' But Doug just hung on to him, yelling, 'I got the thief, I caught the thief!' "

GEORGE HALAS (Owner/Head Coach, Chicago Bears): "One night a fan phoned saying Atkins was cutting up, drunk at a bar. I drove over. Doug saw me enter and shouted a tumultuous river of profanities. I walked up to him and countered with a barrage that, for volume and variety, made his assault a peaceful brook compared to my Niagara. Doug put down his glass and came to camp. At ten minutes before nine in the morning he was out there on the field with no trace of foggy-headedness or wobbly limbs."

RICHIE PETITBON (Defensive Back): "At training camp Doug liked to listen to country music at night, and he'd invite certain guys up to listen to the music. He always kept a Coca-Cola cooler filled with beer in his room, and after the Halas incident, all the coaches were afraid to go check his room. Doug was hurt at the time and didn't have to practice, but the rest of us guys did. Anyway, this one year he had this pit bull at camp, named Rebel. I remember being in there one night, and I said, 'Doug, I got to go to the bathroom.' I was going to slip out, and as I got up to go to the door, Rebel, the dog, starts growling. You know when those pit bulls bite you, they never let you go. I ended up having to piss out the window. No one could leave until Doug, or Rebel, said it was okay to go."

DOUG ATKINS (Defensive End): "This writer one time wrote

an article about me, saying I was washed up. I had some injuries at the time, so I wasn't real upset about it, but I asked the writer why he would write such an article. I told him he couldn't judge the game unless he was in the meetings, watched the movies with us. I said we play the game and we don't understand it, so how could he possibly understand it to write such an article?' He said, 'I played a little football, and I know enough about it. Besides, this is my own personal opinion.' I said, 'That's fine, but I know all the players in the NFL and certainly here with the Bears, and if I see another article that is a bunch of bull in the papers, I'm going to tell everybody in the league that you're a queer. I don't know whether you are or not, but that's just my personal opinion.' "

TOM FEARS (Coach, New Orleans Saints): "They threw away the mold when they made Doug. There will never be another one like him."

Bill George

Guys like Sam Huff and Joe Schmidt got most of the attention because they played with teams that were always in contention. But George was the best as far as I was concerned. He brought all the present romance and charisma to the middle linebacker position.
—Abe Gibron, former teammate and coach

Before there was Dick Butkus, Mike Singletary, or Brian Urlacher, there was Bill George. Born October 27, 1930, in Waynesburg, Pennsylvania, of Syrian descent, he was taught early in life that only the toughest survive in this world. Always very active in sports, George went on to become an All-American in football and wrestling at Wake Forest. Following his senior year, he was selected by the Bears in the second round of the 1951 college draft. Displaying tremendous quickness for a 6'2", 237-pound man, he was moved to middle guard in training camp, where he blossomed in Chicago's 5–2 defense.

In a game a few years later against the Philadelphia Eagles, the Bears were getting beaten by a series of short passes. George, always

Bill George. Courtesy of Chicago Bears.

the student of the game, told defensive captain George Conner that if he didn't have to always line up on the line of scrimmage and pop the center, he could shut down those short passes across the middle. Conner told him to try it. On the next play George lined up three yards behind the line of scrimmage and intercepted the pass. From that day on he was the middle linebacker on the Bears' defense.

George went on to become All-Western Conference in 1955 and 1956, finally winning All-NFL honors in 1957. Tough, mean, George was always prepared, keeping meticulous notes on players and teams. He prided himself in knowing all the Bears' defensive positions, and would be in a teammate's face if he thought they were not prepared to play.

MAURY YOUMANS (Defensive End): "My first exhibition game as a rookie, Doug Atkins and I got to the quarterback at the same time. Doug always had his head down when he got to the quarterback. I rushed a little higher, but the quarterback ducked, and Doug hits me right in the stomach. I'm laying there on the ground. I just can't get up. Our trainer, Ed Rozy, runs out and says, 'You just stay down. Relax for a minute.' He's pulling my belt. Now I'm just a rookie, and Bill George comes up to me and says, 'Maury, are you all right?' I said, 'Yes, I'm all right.' He says, 'Well, you son of a bitch, get up and get in the huddle.' He was one tough guy."

BILL WADE (Quarterback): "Bill George was a super athlete. He could get in the line and be a defensive lineman, as well as linebacker. I mean, who does that today? . . . Nobody. His ability to become a lineman was a tremendous advantage to the Bears' defense. He was a tough guy, no question about that."

Late in 1961, George was hurt in an automobile accident. Never recovering fully, he played the entire 1962 season with intense pain in his neck, resulting in a subpar season. Going into 1963, Bill George felt he had something to prove. His performance in 1962 was not up to his standards, and he was determined to again be that destructive force in the middle of the Bears' defense in 1963.

RICK CASARES (Fullback): "Bill George was the best middle linebacker in the game when he played. He was tough, he was smart, and he could run. People don't realize how fast he was. Bill was a great player. I had great respect for him."

MAURY YOUMANS (Defensive End): "At the end of training camp he gathered the defense together and said, 'Boys, you can listen to the coaches all week, but on Sunday I'll tell you what to do on the field.' He knew the defenses better than anyone, including the coaches."

ED O'BRADOVICH (Defensive End): "John Unitas said one time that he only feared one man in the NFL, and that man was Bill

George. Not because of his physical prowess but because of his mental approach to football. Bill had such great knowledge and such great insight—he was a walking encyclopedia out there. He had a photographic memory, and he would know what all the other teams' tendencies were. I can't tell you how many times that Bill would help me in games. We had a 'sixty-one defensive set,' where we played the right tackle nose-to-nose. The tackle was nose-to-nose with the guard, and I remember Bill hollering to me before the snap, 'Get inside, get inside, come inside.' I went inside, and he made me look like a hero. That's why he's in the Hall of Fame. You could not fool Bill, that was his great strength—his mental toughness and his knowledge of the game."

LEO GEORGE (Bill George's son): "I can remember my dad spending hour after hour in our basement going over films of the opponents. He would study the other teams' tendencies—anything he could pick up on film. He would do it for hours and hours. Clark Shaughnessy was the coach he most admired. He said he was a genius."

STAN JONES (Defensive Tackle): "Bill George was very superstitious. When he and I were captains, we would go out for the coin flip before the game. Someone mentioned to me that one of Bill's superstitions was that he had to be the first one off of the field after the coin flip. So the next game, when it came time to shake hands with the opposing team captains, a plan was put in place. I would reach out and shake hands with the captain in front of Bill, which would cut him off from the other captain. Then I would shake hands really quick with the other captain and then beat him off the field. It drove him crazy. I would come off the field, and Bill would be in hot pursuit. Everybody would be yelling. It looked like we were sky-high for the game, when we were really trying to piss Bill George off about being so damn superstitious."

DOUG ATKINS (Defensive End): "Bill George was a hell of a football player. One time up in Milwaukee, in a real nice hotel, he got up in the middle of the night and was walking down the hall buck naked. Now Bill didn't drink. Oh, he might have a beer once in a while, but he wasn't drunk or anything. Some poor salesman had left his door open. Bill walks in, sits down on the bed. Finally, after a minute, he looks at the salesman and screams, 'Get off of my bed.' The salesman ran out scared for his life. Evidently, Bill had taken a pain killer and was walking in his sleep."

LEO GEORGE (Bill George's son): "My cousin and brother shared a room in our home. My dad wasn't too pleased with the way they were keeping their room, so one time during the winter, my father came upstairs and their room was a mess. He said to them, 'Fine, if you can't keep your room any cleaner than that, get down to the basement.' Walking down to the basement where the furnace was, it was actually warmer than the second floor. My brother says to my cousin, 'Hey, this is better than we had it!' My father heard that, and he put them out back in the shed with the dogs. There was a little gas heater in the shed, and he told them both to get out there."

Mike DITKA

TIGHT END

Doug Atkins came in late and wasn't even quiet about it. He came in, bang, boom, making a racket. He then went down and banged on the Old Man's door. The Old Man was scared to death of Doug. Doug went in the room and closed the door. He leaned up against it and wouldn't let the Old Man out. He was arguing with him for more than hour, not leaving, and keeping the old man up. It was probably close to two in the morning before he left. He drove Halas absolutely nuts. I mean, he used to drive the Old Man crazy. The Old Man wasn't really scared of anybody but Doug. He liked Doug, but he didn't know how to handle him."

John Johnson corrals a Packer. Courtesy of John Johnson.

Green Bay Packers

*About five minutes before one game with Green Bay,
Halas knocked on the door of the Packers' training
room and asked to speak to Vince Lombardi.
Lombardi came to the door, and Halas told him,
"Coach, I hope you have your team ready because
we're going to kick your ass."*

The Green Bay Packers' power sweep, their signature play in the early 1960s, was symbolic of the power football being played in the NFL during that time. The brainchild of Green Bay coach Vince Lombardi, its foundation was traced back to the 1930s and single-wing football. Lombardi, as a member of Fordham's "Seven Blocks of Granite," was impressed with certain aspects of the single-wing offense. He especially liked the way Jock Sutherland, the coach for the University of Pittsburgh, ran his sweeps, utilizing interesting guard-pulling techniques. As he developed his own personal coaching style, Lombardi continued to refine the sweep, keeping the elements of the single wing he liked and incorporating them into his T-formation offense. Focusing on execution rather than deception, his teams attacked defenses with a vengeance.

In his very first meeting with his players in 1959, he explained how important the sweep would be to their success. "Gentlemen, if we can make this play work, we can run the football. If we can run the football, we will win." The Packers would practice that play over and over until it was run with perfection.

DON MCCAFFERTY (Head Coach, Baltimore Colts): "That sweep worked because everybody on that team did his job. It was merely execution, and the opposing defenses got executed. Mysterious? Not a chance. Just too damn good."

VINCE LOMBARDI (Head Coach, Green Bay Packers): "There can never be enough emphasis on repetition. I want my players to be able to run this sweep in their sleep. If we call the sweep twenty times, I'll expect it to work twenty times . . . not eighteen . . . not nineteen. We do it often enough in practice so that no excuse can exist for screwing it up."

Chicago's defensive coordinator, George Allen, was well aware of the sweep, along with the rest of the Packer plays. On a Halas mandate, he and his defensive assistants had spent many hours in the off-season breaking down the Packers' offense. Each play was charted, with special attention given to its frequency, and its effectiveness against the Bears' defense in 1962. All week prior to the Green Bay game, the defense was drilled on each player doing his job, maintaining their positions, staying in their respective lanes. New defensive cocaptain Joe Fortunato would have the added responsibility of calling the defensive plays. If the Bears were going to be successful slowing down the Green Bay offense, the defense must be in the correct defensive positions.

By midweek of the Green Bay game, the Bears decided to place defensive end Ed O'Bradovich and halfback Billy Martin on injured reserve. O'Bradovich, who was still suffering from a heart ailment, and Martin, who had a fractured leg, would not be eligible to play for a minimum of four weeks. By placing them on injured reserve, they would not count against the regular season roster of thirty-seven active players.

George Halas, in his weekly press conference, expressed his concerns to the media about playing the Packers so early in the season. "The Packers are stronger than last year except for the loss of Paul

Hornung's kicking. We're playing the champions and we know it. What else needs to be said?"

Vince Lombardi countered Halas's comments by being extremely complimentary of this Bears team. "They are a much better football team. Their whole system is much simpler than it was a year ago. There is no question that they are a more effective team." But the Packers' head coach made it clear that his team would be ready for the Bears. "Consciously or unconsciously, we've been looking forward to the Bears for two weeks. We will be ready to play."

Adding to the Bears' challenge was the fact that the Packers would come into the game much healthier. Their only banged-up player was defensive tackle Dave Hanner; he had stitches under his eye but was still slated to start on Sunday against the Bears. In all seven NFL games played that week, the Bears were the longest shot to win.

A record crowd of 42,327 fans turned out on September 15, 1963, to watch Green Bay open the regular season at home, against their bitter rival, the Chicago Bears. The Packers, having defeated the Bears eight straight times, were a solid eight-point favorite to win the contest. Exchanging punts to open up the game, each team's defenses held the opponent to no first downs.

On its second possession, Green Bay made the first mistake of the game. As the team attempted to run their power sweep, fullback Jim Taylor was hit behind the line of scrimmage by Bears linebacker Larry Morris and fumbled. Closing from his corner position, Richie Petitbon dove on the loose pigskin at the Packer 41-yard line, giving the Bears good field position.

On first down, Bill Wade hit Ronnie Bull on a short swing pass for a 3-yard gain. After a Joe Marconi dive off-tackle went for 1 yard, Wade went back to Bull on another swing pass. Catching the ball 2 yards behind the line of scrimmage, Bull tried to cut back but was knocked down by Packer middle linebacker Ray Nitschke, a yard shy of the first down. Facing fourth and one from the Packer 32-yard line, Halas went for the field goal. Rookie kicker Bob Jencks split the uprights, giving the Bears an early 3–0 lead.

The Packers returned the kickoff to their own 29-yard line, and quarterback Bart Starr completed two straight passes to move the ball near midfield. After Jimmy Taylor turned the corner for 8 yards, Starr hit Ron Kramer over the middle for a first down at the Bears' 35-yard line. The Bears' defense stiffened, and Green Bay had to settle for a 41-yard Jerry Kramer field goal, to knot the game at 3–3. That ended the scoring for the first half. The Bears' offense was able to move the ball against the Green Bay defense, but still had only three points to show for their efforts. The Packers on offense had turned the ball over three times. Halas was pleased with the way the game was unfolding, but knew if the Bears were going to upset the Packers, his offense would have to score some points.

At the beginning of the second half, the Bears' offense went right to work. Deftly mixing swing passes with runs, Wade steadily moved his team down the field. Reaching the Packer 2-yard line, Packer defensive tackle Dave "Hawg" Hanner broke through the line, stripping Wade of the ball. Green Bay recovered the loose ball, stopping the Bears' drive. Chicago had wasted a golden opportunity to score a touchdown.

Later, in the third period, after once again exchanging punts, the Packers went to the air. Starr's pass bounced off Boyd Dowler's hands, into the arms of Bears safety Roosevelt Taylor. Taylor returned the interception to the Packer 32-yard line, giving the Bears' offense great field position.

On first down Wade faked a handoff to fullback Joe Marconi, then dropped back and floated a spiral toward the back of the end zone to left end John Farrington. Getting behind Packer defender Willie Wood, Farrington angled toward the corner of the end zone, where he made a leaping catch just as he and Wood collided. After a momentary hesitation, the back judge signaled that Farrington had caught the pass out-of-bounds . . . no touchdown. On the Chicago sidelines George Halas went berserk. He charged onto the playing field where he screamed obscenities at referee Art McNally. McNally, without changing expression, looked at Halas and screamed, "Second down!" Halas, shaking his head in disgust, slowly retreated to the Bears' bench. Bill Wade, confident about the play, decided to go back to Farrington again. Hitting him in stride, Farrington was knocked out-of-bounds at the Packer 2-yard line.

Halas on the sideline knew this might be the game right here. His jaw set, the old man thought to himself, 'We may never have this chance again.' Chicago came up to the line, with Farrington split out wide to the left and Johnny Morris split wide to the right. Wade, under center, sent Bull in motion as he called out the signals. Taking the snap from Mike Pyle, he turned and handed off to fullback Joe Marconi. Up front both lines crashed forward. The game, so hard fought, might be settled here. The Packer linemen went low to the ground, digging, scratching, trying desperately to push the Bears' offensive line backward. Bears linemen Bob Wetoska, Jim Cadile, Ted Karras, and Roger Davis and center Mike Pyle met the challenge. With their legs churning, they pushed forward with all the strength they could muster. Marconi, hitting a wall of humanity, had nowhere to go. Instinctively spinning around, the burly fullback continued to push forward. Finally he felt the line move forward, and with one final effort he pushed his way into the end zone for the touchdown. Chicago had scored perhaps their biggest touchdown in seven long years. Jencks's extra point put the Bears on top 10–3.

The Packers tried desperately to rally, but the Bears' defense answered every challenge. Interceptions by Bill George and Dave Whitsell finally sealed the victory for the Bears. Chicago had humbled the mighty Packers in Green Bay. It was only one game into the season, but the Chicago Bears had gotten a big monkey off their backs.

"Gentlemen," George Halas told his team following the game, "this is the greatest team effort in the history of the Chicago Bears." Captain Joe Fortunato decided that, in honor of such a great win, they would give one of the game balls to the old man. His teammates felt that the first-year captain had also earned one. "Joe called a hell of a game," declared defensive tackle Stan Jones. "He put us in the right spot all the time." Bill George echoed Jones's sentiments. "Joe did a tremendous job. He set me up for my interception in the fourth quarter. He forced Ron Kramer to the inside, and all I had to do was catch the pass."

Joe Fortunato. Courtesy of Joe Fortunato.

Over in the Packers' locker room, a quiet Vince Lombardi felt that too many turnovers had killed his team's chance of winning. "Actually we didn't play bad defensively, but we were awfully inconsistent on offense. When you give up the ball as often as we did. You get beat." A dejected Bart Starr added, "When you give up four interceptions, you don't deserve to win."

The Bears outgained the Packers in total yards 231 to 150. Bill Wade had connected on 18 of 34 passes, for 124 yards. The Chicago defense, well prepared by George Allen, made no substitutions the entire game. Up in the stands, Clark Shaughnessy, who had flown in from the West Coast, was duly impressed. "The Bears beat the Packers thoroughly, both on offense and on defense. The Bears deserved to win."

JOE FORTUNATO (Linebacker): "That was a great defensive game. We played a great game, and we just knocked the crap out of them."

BOYD DOWLER (Flanker, Green Bay Packers): "I just dropped that pass. I plain missed it. Lombardi never said a word to me about me missing that one, and I can assure you I didn't bring it up."

CHUCK MATHER (Coach): "The old man said to me before the season, 'Chuck, I want you to put together some plays that will be exclusively for Green Bay. We will practice them once a week during preseason.' I said, 'Coach, you can't do that.' He said, 'That's what we are going to do.' So I put together the plays, and looking back it wasn't the plays that mattered . . . what mattered was once a week the emphases would be on Green Bay. This put the motivation in the players that we were doing something special to beat Green Bay."

WILLIE WOOD (Defensive Back, Green Bay Packers): "All of our games against the Bears were thrilling. It didn't matter what the Bears' or Packers' records were when we played, you knew it was going to be a fistfight the whole time. The best team didn't always win, and if you were not careful, you could get hurt."

George Halas savored this great win all the way back to Chicago, but Papa Bear knew that starting tomorrow, it was time to get ready for the Minnesota Vikings. Over the years the Vikings had proven to be a tough foe, especially with Fran Tarkenton at quarterback. Halas didn't want the euphoria of this great win to get in the way of the Bears' preparation. The old coach pushed his seat back, closed his eyes, and muttered to himself, "No way are the Vikings going to beat us next week. No way."

Bears versus Minnesota. Courtesy of Rick Casares.

Minnesota Vikings

In 1961, the Minnesota Vikings opened their first season in the NFL at home against the Chicago Bears. Viking head coach Norm Van Brocklin decided that his quarterback that day would be the veteran George Shaw. Although the Vikings' coach saw great promise in rookie Fran Tarkenton, he felt his young player was not seasoned enough to become the starter. Van Brocklin, who was a legend at quarterback in the NFL, had through necessity become the traditional pocket passer. Slow afoot, but possessing a great arm as a player, the Dutchman had little tolerance for quarterbacks that did not stay in the pocket. In preseason games Tarkenton was brilliant at times, but he frustrated his coach with his scrambling around. Van Brocklin decided to bring the kid from Georgia along slowly, teaching him the proper way to play the position.

A crowd of 32,236 packed Metropolitan Stadium on a beautiful fall day in 1961 to watch their team's first-ever regular season game. After a scoreless first quarter, the Vikings kicked a field goal to take an early 3–0 lead. Following an interception, Minnesota squandered a second chance to score, as the Bears' defense repeatedly sacked Shaw, finally forcing him to the sidelines with a shoulder injury. Van Brocklin, now through necessity, inserted the young rookie into the game. Tarkenton, able to avoid the Bears' pass rush, quickly moved his team down the field, scoring the game's first touchdown on a rollout pass. When the game was finished, Tarkenton had completed 17 of 23 passes, four of them for touchdowns, as the Vikings upset the Bears 37–13. A star was born in Minnesota.

Losing to the upstart Vikings was difficult for George Halas. The Bears, so rich in tradition, had been defeated by an expansion team in its very first game. From that day forward, Halas knew that preparing to stop Fran Tarkenton called for a supreme effort from him, his coaching staff, and all of his defensive players. The Vikings would not catch the Bears unprepared again.

ANGELO COIA (Flanker): "When Tarkenton came in and starting running around, the defense had their tongues hanging out by the third quarter. At halftime the Vikings gave Halas a little bear cub, and when they started beating us pretty bad in the second half, Halas kicked the cub in the ass and the people started booing us."

MAURY YOUMANS (Defensive End): "We could not get up for that game in 1961. We just didn't have any respect for them, being an expansion team. Even during the game it was hard to believe what was happening. Fran Tarkenton just took over that game."

Opening the 1963 season with a 24–20 comeback win over San Francisco, the Vikings were sky-high going into the Bears contest. Losing twice last year to the Bears, the Vikings were looking forward to exacting some revenge on their Western Conference opponent. They were hopeful the Bears would still be celebrating the win over the Packers. "Keep telling those Bears how great they are, would you?" Van Brocklin told the Chicago press. "We were very impressed by the Bears victory over Green Bay Sunday. I think everybody in the league welcomed it with the exception of the Packers. It was the best thing that could have happened to our league. Now all the teams feel they have a chance including us. The door is definitely open. But that doesn't mean I expect Green Bay to fold. We've been looking at the movies and they simply got whipped. They got hit and they couldn't recover."

The Dutchman was slowly building the Vikings into a contender. Former Bears fullback Bill Brown and halfback Tommy Mason were becoming outstanding running backs, operating behind an improving offensive line, centered by Mick Tinglehoff. Van Brocklin, pleased with the way his offense was progressing, also had high expectations for rookie flanker Paul Flatley. The young receiver out of Northwestern had been sensational in training camp, and the Viking coach felt that the youngster could become a real force in the league.

Linebacker Rip Hawkins and defensive end Jim Marshall were leaders on a young, aggressive Viking defense. The Vikings were headed in the right direction.

Following the Green Bay game, the Bears went back to work to prepare for a tough battle against the Vikings. The Bears' head coach promised a few surprises. "We have some things in mind. Anytime you face a quarterback like Tarkenton that moves around like he does, you need to alter your game plan. We will do just that." Other than that statement, Halas remained quiet the rest of the week.

The game on Sunday began with the Bears' defense again creating an early turnover. Minnesota on their opening drive had reached the Bears' 45-yard line. Tommy Mason, trying to run right, was hit hard by Bill George and fumbled. The ball popped up in the air and was grabbed by safety Roosevelt Taylor, who scampered 29 yards to the Viking 26-yard line, giving the Bears great field position. After Ronnie Bull ran off-tackle for 2 yards, Bill Wade faked a dive to Marconi, then hit Bull out in the flat with a pass. Sidestepping one defender, Bull out-ran two Viking players to the end zone. Bob Jencks's kick gave the Bears a quick 7–0 lead.

Throughout the remainder of the first quarter, the Vikings' offense was held in check by the Bears' aggressive defense. On offense Chicago had chances to put points on the board, but rookie kicker Bob Jencks missed two field goal attempts. Early in the second quarter, the Vikings reached the Bears' 20-yard line. After an interference penalty moved the ball back 15 yards, Tarkenton hit tight end Jerry Reichel in the corner of the end zone for a touchdown. The Vikings had tied it at seven apiece.

Later in the second period, Bears cornerback Dave Whitsell, intercepted a Tarkenton pass but fumbled as he hit the ground. Vikings fullback Bill Brown scooped up the loose ball and returned it 20 yards, before being knocked out-of-bounds by Bill George. Linebacker Larry

Morris, protesting that Whitsell was down when he fumbled, shoved an official and was ejected from the game. Referee Harry Brubaker decided his crew needed to discuss this decision further. After much deliberation it was decided Whitsell was down when he fumbled, giving Chicago the ball back. The Bears, now minus one great linebacker, had possession at the Viking 35-yard line.

After two running plays netted five yards, Bill Wade found Mike Ditka wide open over the middle. Refusing to go down, Ditka knocked two Viking defenders to the ground, scoring the touchdown. The Bears led at the half 14–7.

The third quarter was hard fought, with neither team able to score. At the beginning of the fourth quarter the Vikings turned the ball over again, when Joe Fortunato recovered Tommy Mason's fumble at the Viking 34-yard line. Six straight running plays advanced the ball to the 1-yard line, where Wade, following the blocks of Bob Wetoska and Mike Pyle, dove into the end zone for the touchdown. Jencks's kick made it 21–7.

The last score of the day was set up by a Rosie Taylor interception at the Vikings' 20-yard line. Bill Wade quickly found Mike Ditka open in the end zone for the Bears' fourth touchdown of the afternoon. The final score was 28–7.

The Bears' second straight win of the season was again keyed by the defense, as they created five turnovers on three pass interceptions and two fumbles. They had allowed just ten points in the first two games.

George Halas breathed a sigh of relief at the game's conclusion. "We came up here with quite a bit of trepidation. This Viking team has a lot of spunk and they showed it in the first quarter. They have a good team and I'm glad we don't have to come back here this year," Halas told the press following the game.

Although complimentary of his defense, Halas singled out the offense and Bill Wade for their play. "He called a splendid game. He was extremely accurate today. He picked the Vikings secondary apart."

The Vikings, as expected, were sullen after the game. They knew that they had had chances but turnovers had killed them. "We beat ourselves with all the mistakes. You just can't give up the ball as we did and win," said a dejected Tarkenton. Statistically, the game was fairly even, with the Bears gaining a total of 359 yards for the game, just 33 yards more than the Vikings' 326. Wade was 23 of 33, for 253 yards, three touchdowns, and no interceptions. Tarkenton did not fare as well, finishing up the day 16–24 for 150 yards, one touchdown, and three interceptions. The Bears' defense now had seven pass interceptions in two games. This second win of the season now behind them, the Bears were already directing their attention to the next week's opponent, the Detroit Lions.

FRAN TARKENTON (Quarterback, Minnesota Vikings): "Doug Atkins is the strongest man in football and also the biggest. When he rushes the passer with those oak tree arms way up in the air, he's twelve feet tall. And if he gets to you, the whole world starts spinning."

Angelo COIA

FLANKER

After one game my second year I wasn't feeling well, so I went home. The next day at the team meeting Halas is walking around the room talking about two young sophomore players who don't care if the team wins or loses. I'm not really paying much attention as it wasn't me. He comes up beside me and hits my play book and knocks it on the floor. He had apparently got me mixed up with somebody else. At that time he had this detective agency following us. He fined me a thousand dollars. If you think of that, I was only making ten thousand dollars for the year. That was one-tenth of my salary—imagine what that fine would be today. Then to top it off, he took it from me on Christmas Day. I had to go meet with him in the morning, and I thought he was going to give me the money back. . . . He didn't.

"One year we were playing San Francisco, and one of our players, Pete Manning, was injured. Halas gave him a 49ers hat and told him to stand on the San Francisco sideline. At halftime Pete says to me, 'I feel crazy over there. I got to root for the 49ers.' Halas grilled him at halftime about what they were saying about us.

"We played an exhibition game up in Canada. On the first series of downs, it was second down and I'm wide open. Our quarterback hits me right in the stomach going right down the middle of the field, and

Angelo Coia. © Brace Photo.

I drop it. I come out of the game, and I'm sitting on the bench, and I see him looking for me. He comes over and slaps me right in the face and says, 'Don't ever do that again.' I felt like two cents.

"My first year the rookies had to report a week before the veterans. Nobody looked particularly big, and we pretty much had the place to ourselves. I'll never forget, they had this box where you could sit and put the powder on your feet, so that the tape didn't stick to your socks. The first day the veterans came in, I'm on this box when it was like the sun got blocked out. I never had seen anybody that big in my life. The first thing I thought was, 'If Doug Atkins ever hits me, he'll kill me.' "

George Halas. Courtesy of Chicago Bears.

7

The Staff

George Allen

During his tenure with the Bears, George Allen wore many hats for the organization. Hired as a scout in 1958, this highly organized young coach impressed Halas with his willingness to work around the clock. No matter what the task, big or small, Allen always had it done on time. In 1960 the AFL began competing against the NFL for players. Undaunted, George Allen became the Bears' point man on negotiations. A tireless worker, he had no equal in signing players.

MAURY YOUMANS (Defensive End): "The night before the 1960 Cotton Bowl, which was my last college game, George Allen comes up to me in the hotel hallway. He said, 'Maury, let's talk a little about signing this contract with the Bears.' I told him I was really interested in seeing what the AFL and the Canadian League had to offer before making any decisions. George says, 'I got a thousand dollar check here. Will you hold this for me?' He says, 'I got to sign something.' I guess he thought I was going to look at a thousand dollars and say, 'Wow! Where do I sign?' After about thirty seconds, he says, 'You know, that check is yours if you sign this contract now. You'll be playing for the Chicago Bears, and it will be the best move you could ever make in your life.' I said, 'Coach, I got a ball game tomorrow. I really

George Allen. Courtesy of Chicago Bears.

don't want to think about anything like that.' He says, 'Okay, go have a good game, and I'll talk to you afterwards.'

"I play the game, we beat Texas, win the National Championship, and I go on to the Senior Bowl. I have a tremendous game there, and now everybody is after me. I'm leaning toward playing in Canada because at that time they paid as well as either the AFL or NFL and I liked the Toronto coach. George Allen is leaving messages everywhere for me, but I'm not answering them, as I had pretty much ruled the Bears out.

"I tell the Toronto coach following the Senior Bowl that I'm very interested in playing for him, but I would like to talk to my folks first. He said, 'Fine, Maury. We'll fly into Syracuse next week.' George Allen keeps calling me, having me paged, but I'm ducking him. I go home and it's set that the coach from Toronto is going to come and meet my parents, and then we were going to talk about signing up. Well, the next morning the phone rings, and it was George Allen. I am at my parents' house, and he said, 'Maury, you had a great game, and I want to get you to sign up with the Bears.' I said, 'Coach, I've already signed with Toronto.' He said, 'Oh, you made a big mistake. You shouldn't have done that.' I said, 'Well, I haven't signed yet.' That is all I needed to say. He said, 'Don't you do anything until I get there.' He said, 'I'm coming in tomorrow and I want to meet you.' So reluctantly I said, 'All right, I'll see you at the university.' Well, there was a bad snowstorm, and the coach from Toronto got stuck in Buffalo and couldn't get into Syracuse. George Allen somehow the next morning got in okay. The first thing he said when he sees me was, 'I want to meet your parents.' The minute we walked in the door he walked right to my mother and said, 'Mrs. Youmans, don't let this boy make a big mistake. He needs to be with the Chicago Bears.' Well, that's all she needed to hear. This handsome, big-time coach wanted her son. I had no chance after that. I had to sign with the Bears. He went over to the telephone and called Coach Halas and had me talk to him. Halas said, 'Kid, you belong with the Bears.' So that's how I ended up signing with the Bears. George Allen wouldn't let up until he signed me."

ROGER DAVIS (Offensive Guard): "When I had finally signed with the Bears, he told us rookies, 'Don't tell the veteran players how much you are making: they'll hate you.' Actually, that was so they didn't know how little we were making."

JOE FORTUNATO (Linebacker): "George Allen was just kind of a flunky with the Bears early on, but he turned out to be one hell of a coach. When he went to the Redskins he wanted me to come with him and play and be a coach. He offered me a big contract to go to Washington. I just didn't want to leave the Bears, and I told him, you know, I just love the Bears. I went in to see Halas, and I told him what was going on. He told me he didn't want me to leave. Halas said, 'If you don't leave, I'll give you a two-year no-cut contract.' I said, 'What the hell is a no-cut contract?' He signed me to a two-year guaranteed contract."

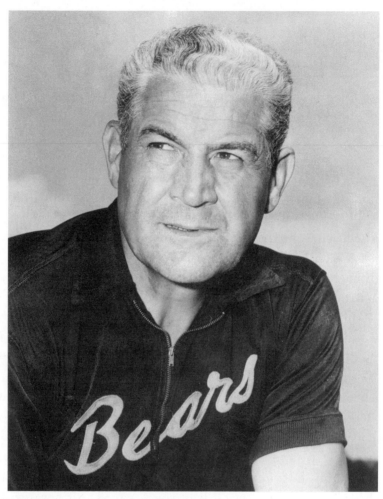

Joe Stydahar. Courtesy of Chicago Bears.

BILL WADE (Quarterback): "George Allen coached with the Los Angeles Rams when I was playing out there, and so I knew him. He was a very nice person and was easy to get along with. He was really dedicated to his work. When we were with the Rams, Allen was younger than the players he coached. Both Tom Fears and Elroy Hirsch were older than him. He could relate to the players. He was a hard worker."

ROOSEVELT TAYLOR (Defensive Back): "He was the reason I was with the Bears. He would always tell Halas when I first got there,

'Give this kid a chance. He's going to be a good one.' George Allen was a great coach."

Joe Stydahar

Chicago's defensive-line coach was a Hall of Fame player for the Bears after being drafted in 1936. This giant of a man (6'4", 245 pounds) was a two-way performer at tackle who had the unique distinction of being one of the last players in the NFL to not wear a helmet. He had a no-nonsense approach to coaching, similar to the way he played the game.

CHUCK MATHER (Coach): "In practice one day I was presenting the opponent's offensive plays to the defense team. I notice that Stydahar is not present. I said to Halas, 'Where's Stydahar?' Halas looks around and spots him up in the stands. He calls him down and asks him what is he doing up in the stands? Stydahar tells Halas he can see better in the stands."

Chuck Mather

Chuck Mather came to the Bears in 1958, as backfield coach and scout. A successful high school coach in Massillon, Ohio, in the 1940s, he came to the Bears from the University of Kansas, where he became head coach in 1954. Voted coach of the year in the Big Eight Conference in 1957, Mather was credited with being the first to use IBM computer printouts in the evaluation of players.

Jim Dooley

Jim Dooley was the Bears' number-one selection in the 1952 college draft. A very competent receiver, he led the Bears in receptions in 1953, 1957, and 1959. Always a student of the game, Dooley's strength as a coach was in the film room, breaking down the opponent's defenses.

ERICH BARNES (Defensive Back, New York Giants): "Jim Dooley in the late 1950s was the best possession receiver in football.

Chuck Mather. Courtesy of Chicago Bears.

Chuck Mather   Best wishes

He could cut on a dime. Today they talk about the passing game like it
is something new. Nothing's new in football. All the years I was around
the game with three teams, nobody has invented anything."

ANGELO COIA (Flanker): "I thought Jim Dooley was as smart a
coach as we had. He would tell me, 'If you want to run certain patterns
in the game, tell Bill Wade to set it up this way.' He was always on the
money every time. It got you the kind of defense you wanted to see,
and if you ran the right kind of pattern you got open. I thought he
would be a great head coach. I don't know what happened because I
wasn't there."

BILL WADE (Quarterback): "Jim Dooley was a coach more than
a player when I was with the Bears. He had a brilliant mind for the
game—the best I have ever been around in analyzing film. When Jim

Jim Dooley. Courtesy of Jim Dooley and Chicago Bears.

Dooley told me something, I could take it to the bank. I had total confidence in him. If he said, 'Run this, . . .' I said okay. I would go out and run whatever he thought would work, and it would work. He knew what he was doing, and he gave me a lot of information. For example, when we played the Packers he told me which way Willie Wood was going to go on certain plays. It had to do with his feet, how he was standing. There was a linebacker who every time he was going to blitz, he'd start moving his feet. There were all kind of things that as I was up to the line of scrimmage and calling signals, I would see thanks to Dooley. All this information would give me a good idea as to what they were going to do when the ball was snapped. Jim studied those movies. We had other assistants there who helped to some degree, but Jim Dooley was the one that I had the most confidence in."

JOE FORTUNATO (Linebacker): "Jim Dooley, he was great in the film room, breaking down and developing a scheme, a strategy, an offense, but coaching and executing—it was difficult for him."

JIM DOOLEY (Coach): "In 1962 Coach Halas called me in and said that they are going to have to let me go as they needed an extra man on the kicking game. He said they had put me on waivers and that the Minnesota Vikings had picked me up. Earlier in the month I had said to him that, when it was all over for me, I would like to come back and coach for him. I said 'I'm easy to get along with, coach, I don't ask for much.' I knew that he would like that. He said yes, so I knew I would have a job later on. When he released me, he said, 'Jim, I don't want you to go up to Minnesota; I want you to start now as a coach. I want you to continue to work out every day, I'll pay you your full salary, I have some projects for you. I want you to go over all the film we have.' So I started with the Green Bay film, the New York Giants film, and the [films of the] Dallas Cowboys, who were a very organized team. It took me all season to do, but I had everything down on what each of those teams did on offense and defense. So when 1963 came coach had me show the team during training camp what I had learned. It helped to better prepare us for the season. I have always been very proud of that."

Sid Luckman

In 1963 Sid Luckman was in his eighth year as quarterback coach. Unlike the rest of the staff, Luckman was a part-time coach, showing up once a week to work with the quarterbacks and receivers. His career as a Bears player was legendary, but his contributions as a coach remain questionable. The Bears players were always respectful of Luckman because of what he had accomplished as a player and his close relationship with George Halas.

Sid Luckman. Courtesy of Chicago Bears.

ANGELO COIA (Flanker): "Luke Johnsos, who was the end coach, and Sid Luckman for some reason didn't get along. They just didn't talk to each other. Sid would come down from Chicago once a week before the second practice during training camp. We would have to be on the field an hour early. He would run us through a practice—just the receivers and the quarterbacks. When he was done, Halas would come out and say, 'Let's warm up.' Us receivers were sitting over there with our tongues hanging out, having run pass patterns for an hour. We say, 'WARM UP! We've been running straight for an hour!' Luke would pretend like Luckman hadn't even been there, like we hadn't done a thing."

BILL WADE (Quarterback): "Sid Luckman kind of worked with

me before the season started. He would come out for what Dooley called 'the Luckman-Day Quarterback-Testing Thing.' Sid wanted to help. But I don't know how much help he was. It's like me trying to give help to Brett Favre today. I mean, what kind of help can I give him? You got to be out there, you got to react to what is happening on the field—that's the most important thing."

Phil Handler

After graduating from Texas in 1930, Handler went on to a fine six-year pro career with the Chicago Cardinals. An outstanding lineman, Handler joined the Bears' staff in 1952. He was in charge of the Bears' offensive line.

MIKE PYLE (Center): "Phil was a wonderful character, a real good guy. We would complain sometimes about Phil doing the scouting reports. One time he referred to Danny Villeuveuna of the Cowboys as Vanilla Wafer. But the greatest story is the one that Bill Bishop told for years. Handler is out at the end of the line during a team scrimmage. He's watching to see how the guys line up, whether they are offsides or not. Phil looks down the line, and he sees Bishop offsides and he screams, 'Bishy, you're lining up across the ball—get back!' Bishop just yelled back, 'Phil, forget it. This isn't a game.' Phil got so mad, he said, 'Bishy, if you don't believe me, come out here and look for yourself.' That's a classic story."

ROGER DAVIS (Offensive Guard): "Phil Handler used to run the projector when the offensive team would watch film. He was old and he would fall asleep. Halas would get to a play and say, 'Phil, run that back.' Well, Phil would be dozing. Halas would scream, 'PHIL, RUN THAT BACK!' All of us in the room would be trying not to laugh."

Luke Johnsos

Luke Johnsos was a real veteran of the staff in 1963, with more than thirty-two years with the Bears as both a player and a coach. In 1942, when George Halas went into the navy, Johnsos was made dual

Luke Johnsos. Courtesy of Chicago Bears.

head coach with Hunk Anderson. He had been part of six championships leading into the 1963 season.

CHUCK MATHER (Coach): "Luke Johnsos was a very good
coach. He was sometimes referred to as the 'Spy in the Sky.' He was the
coach in the press box that would send the plays down. He called a play
that may have won the championship for us. We were down on the 10-
yard line, and he called this play for Ditka. I said at the time no, because
in a goal-line offense, the defense always stuffs the tight end. In calling
that play I felt that Ditka would never get out. Johnsos kept insisting
we call this play. Finally I sent it in and Mike was smart enough to move
out about three yards, and the defensive guy didn't go out with him.

Ed Rozy. Courtesy of Chicago Bears.

So he caught the pass that went to the 1-yard line. Then Bill Wade scored on my favorite play, the quarterback sneak."

Ed Rozy

Ed Rozy joined the Bears as trainer in 1948. A protégé of famed trainer Matt Bullock, he came to the Bears from Marquette University, where besides being a trainer, he coached boxing, wrestling, and fencing.

MIKE PYLE (Center): "Ed Rozy was a real character. He wasn't highly trained. He was the kind of guy that just learned his trade on the job and was pretty funny about it. Every time my ankle hurt, he just put more tape on it. That was the treatment—just put more tape on it."

ED O'BRADOVICH (Defensive End): "You could go to him and tell him you were not feeling good. The first thing out of his mouth was, 'How many salt pills are you taking?' I'd tell him I was taking two a day. He'd say, 'It's not enough . . . take six a day.' Then you come to him and say, 'I'm not feeling good.' 'What's the matter? You a little weak, a little sweaty? How many salt pills you taking?' 'I'm taking six a day.' 'That's too many. Take two.' He was something else."

RICK CASARES (Fullback): "Ed and I got along great until one day I put soap powder in one of his whirlpool baths."

CHUCK MATHER (Coach): "Ed Rozy used to listen to what the players talked about in the training room and go tell Halas. I didn't like that because I felt there were some things that Halas didn't need to know."

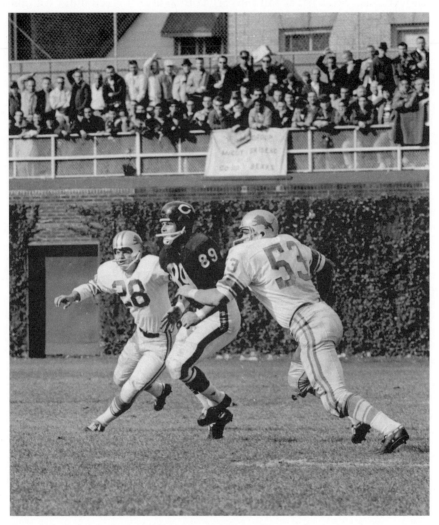

Ditka vs. Lions. Courtesy of Ron Nelson/Prairie Street Art.

Detroit Lions

Undefeated through the first two games of the 1963 season, the Bears would be on the road for the third straight week, traveling to the Motor City to play the Detroit Lions. The injury list continued to grow, with starting defensive tackle Fred Williams lost for at least six weeks with a shoulder separation. Adding to the problem was the health of Joe Fortunato, whose leg had stiffened up against the Vikings. His status for Sunday's game with the Lions was questionable.

Detroit, home or away, was always a tough game for the Bears, so Halas prepared accordingly. A main concern for him was the Detroit defense, which had not allowed the Bears to score a touchdown in the last three games played between the two teams. These two Western Conference foes last season had split the two games between them, with each winning at home.

Detroit's strength, similar to the Bears, was their defense. After finishing second to the Packers last year with a record of 11–3, the Lions felt they had the talent to go all the way in 1963. Led by All-Pro middle linebacker Joe Schmidt, the Lion defense was bolstered by a great defensive backfield, which included Dick "Night Train" Lane, Yale Lary, and Dick Labeau. Up front, big Roger Brown, Floyd Peters, and Sam Williams provided an outstanding pass rush, but the Lions would be forced to play the entire season minus their All-Pro defensive tackle,

Alex Karras. Karras had been suspended by NFL commissioner Pete Rozelle for gambling. A tough, physical player, Karras always spelled trouble for the Bears' offensive line.

ROGER DAVIS (Offensive Guard): "Alex Karras was something else to play against. The veterans had warned me, the first time I played against him as a rookie, to watch out for his quickness. The way the first game went was our defense scored on an interception, then we scored on offense, so we were up two touchdowns and didn't have to pass. That was his great thing—pass rushing. After the game I thought he was not that tough. Well, the next time we played them it went the opposite way—we got behind. Now forced to pass every play, I couldn't even find him, much less block him. I was holding him like heck, and I was tackling him when he was getting by me. He was getting madder and madder. Finally Halas put his brother [Ted] in the game to see if he could stop him. The first play, Ted went low on him. He thought it was me and kicked him. Alex couldn't see very well and didn't wear contacts when he played. He kicked his own brother in the head. He was a tough player."

The Lions had opened the 1963 season with a 23–2 win over the Los Angeles Rams, but were soundly beaten by Green Bay the preceding Sunday, 31–10. Quarterback Milt Plum, off to a slow start, was completing only 41 percent of his passes, which ranked him near the bottom of the league in quarterback ratings. Last year veteran quarterback Earl Morrall had split time with Plum, but had been used sparingly so far in the early going. Running backs Nick Pietrosante, Danny Lewis, and rookie Larry Ferguson were all off to a slow start, as the Lions were having problems rushing the football. The Detroit offense needed to rebound against the tough Bears defense, which gave George Allen grave concerns. "This is the type of team that might break out suddenly. We have been trying to guard against every possibility, including the chance that they may use some different formations against us."

Detroit could ill-afford to let the Bears get too far ahead of them in the standings, which made this a "must-win" game for them.

Because of the past history of great games between these two teams, George Halas in no way was going to let his team take the Lions lightly. "The Packers were lucky to beat the Lions," Halas told the press. "After watching the films of that game, you can't have any other impression. The score doesn't indicate anything at all, it really doesn't. It was a tight struggle. The Packers got all the breaks and the Lions will be fired up on Sunday against us. They will be looking for some of those breaks to go their way."

The Bears' defense, although banged up, seemed to be better prepared this year, allowing only ten points through two games. The improved play caught the eye of the Chicago media.

DICK HACKENBERG (Sportswriter, *Chicago Sun-Times*): "There has to be something more than sheer coincidence in the fact that, in retrospect, the improvement in the Bears defenses dates back to the entrusting of these departmental duties to George Allen. The addition of Joe Stydahar to the coaching staff has helped tighten the screws."

Midweek, Chicago activated John Johnson to shore up their depleted defensive roster. The 6'5", 260-pound tackle had been placed on the taxi squad at the end of the exhibition season. Johnson had impressed the entire coaching staff with his strength and quickness. Initially signed as an offensive tackle, he had been moved to defense. With Stan Jones and Earl Leggett the only other healthy defensive tackles, Johnson was a much needed addition.

JOHN JOHNSON (Defensive End): "At the end of preseason in 1963, after our last practice, Ed Rozy comes up and says, 'Coach wants to see you. Bring your playbook.' I was devastated because I thought I had played well during the exhibition games. I knew that when Rozy told you to see coach and bring your playbook, you're on your way out. I'm sitting in the locker room, and I suddenly remembered the coach of Ottawa, in the Canadian League, had told me, if it doesn't work out with the Bears, give him a call. So I call the guy from the locker room before I go in to see Halas and explain the situation. He tells me to come up; they have ten games left in the season. He would pay me a thousand dollars a game, which was basically what my Bears contract was for. I go in and see Halas, and he says, 'Kid, we're going to have a great team this year, but we're only going to keep two rookies, and you're not one of them.' I told him I was disappointed about not making the team, as I thought I had played well. He says, 'Kid, we're going to keep you on the taxi squad and pay you $7,500.' I said, 'But my contract is for $10,000.' Halas says, 'Well, we don't pay anybody that. We will only pay $7,500.' I told him my wife's pregnant and we really needed the money. He said, 'You're a good Catholic kid. We will give you $8,000, but don't tell anybody . . . but not one cent more.' I said, 'I appreciate that, Coach, but I really need the money. Besides, if somebody got hurt, you would probably activate me first because you were paying me more money.' He says, 'You know what, kid, you got a good business mind . . . $8,500 and that's it.' I told him that I appreciated what he offered, but I had talked with the coach in Canada, and he was willing to pay me the $10,000. He says, 'Go to Canada . . . but just remember your family who lives in Indiana. . . . They will never get to see you play, unless you get to the Grey Cup. I can assure you, kid, that would be the only time a Canadian game would be shown on TV here. Go ahead . . . go on up there.' I said, 'Thanks, Mr. Halas, for the opportunity. Here is your playbook,' and I walked out. I'm walking down this long hallway when Halas yells out the door, 'I'll give you 9,500 bucks and not a cent more.' I turned around and said, 'I'll take it.' "

Bill Wade, off his strong performance against Minnesota, was now ranked second in passing in the league, trailing only New York's Y. A. Tittle. Wade had completed forty-one of fifty-six passes attempted so far this season. Tight end Mike Ditka and halfback Ronnie Bull each had caught nine passes through two games. The offense understood they would need to score some points Sunday against a very tough Detroit defense.

On Sunday against Detroit, the Bears came out smoking on both sides of the ball to begin the game. The offense, behind the brilliant passing of Bill Wade, scored four touchdowns in the first half alone. The Bears' defense, not to be outdone, shut the Lions out in the first thirty minutes of the game and scored a touchdown on a Richie Petitbon 64-yard interception return.

Trailing 35–0 to start the second half, Detroit rallied for three touchdowns behind backup quarterback Earl Morrall, but it was too little, too late. The Bears held on for a convincing 37–21 win.

Chicago improved their record to 3–0, while the Lions fell to 1–2. The offense had taken a major step forward in completely dominating a very good Detroit defense in the first half. Bill Wade, besides running for one score, tossed touchdown passes to Angelo Coia, Johnny Morris, and Mike Ditka. The veteran quarterback called a masterful game, utilizing long counts to keep Detroit's aggressive front four off balance. Considering the trouble the Bears' offense had in recent games, this was a great performance by this much maligned unit.

On defense Doug Atkins had a sensational game, sacking Morrall for a safety and harassing Lion quarterbacks all game long. The defense, with the team way ahead, played more conservatively in the second half, giving up a season-high twenty-one points. Although this was more than the team had given up in the first two games combined, the players overall were pleased with their performance. "We did what we needed to do today," said Bill George in the Bears' locker room. "The Lions never gave up, but we always felt we controlled the game."

Coach Halas was pleased that his team had now beaten two of the best teams in football on the road. It had been a long time since a Bears team had accomplished that. It was a good start to what everyone hoped would be a great season.

RONNIE BULL (Halfback): "We used to have the pregame meals, and the guys were sick of just steak and potatoes, high—protein food, and wanted something different. Some of the guys asked for eggs and pancakes, stuff like that to eat. So they're talking, and they asked if there was anything else somebody would like to have to eat. J. C. says, 'Why don't we have something good, like hot dogs and chili?' J. C. was a funny guy."

Johnny Unitas. Courtesy of Ron Nelson/Prairie Street Art.

Baltimore Colts

The Bears came home 3–0, all alone in first place in the Western Conference. Monday was spent moving into the Wrigley Field locker room, now vacated by the Cubs with the baseball season completed. Manager Bob Kennedy's ball club once again finished in the second division, seventeen games behind the pennant-winning Los Angeles Dodgers. On the other side of town, the White Sox had fared better, winning ninety-two games in 1963, but finished second to the New York Yankees, some ten games behind in the standings.

George Halas was looking forward to finally playing before the home folks on Sunday. This week's opponent, the Baltimore Colts, was two games behind the Bears in the West, with a 1–2 record. Losing their home opener 37–21 to the New York Giants, the Colts rebounded on the road, beating San Francisco 20–14. This past week, traveling to Green Bay, the Colts lost 31–20.

Johnny Unitas, the Colts' veteran quarterback, always seemed to play well against the Bears. Over the years Unitas had defeated the Bears with some last-minute heroic finishes. Halas had great respect for the Colts' quarterback, and he summed up his feelings about facing him. "You always have to worry about Johnny Unitas. The Colts are never out of a game with him in there. We are going to have to play well against them this week, if we're going to have a chance to win. No lead is safe with that guy out there. He runs the clock better than any-body. He always worries me."

Baltimore approached the game with the possibility of playing without their great receiver, Raymond Berry. Having injured his leg in the loss to the Packers, Berry's status for Sunday's clash against the Bears was doubtful. With or without Berry, the Colts' passing attack with Unitas at the helm was as good as there was in the NFL.

DAN SULLIVAN (Offensive Tackle, Baltimore Colts): "Johnny Unitas always insisted that all the interior linemen know each receiver's pass routes, so you could vary your style, so you were not sitting back all the time just pass blocking. Sometimes you could go after a guy. He would always say to us, 'Make sure you guys know what are the short routes, what are the intermediate routes, and what are the long routes. Then when I need you for only three seconds on the quickies, you can change your style up and go after the guy.' It was important to our passing game that we all knew the passing routes. Occasionally he would quiz you to keep you on your toes. He'd ask us, 'How much time do I need on a certain pass?' He was great that way."

The Bears had swept the Colts the past two years, winning all four games played between the two teams. Halas and the staff, concerned that the players might become complacent, worked the team hard in preparation for Sunday's game.

On offense the Bears, led by Bill Wade's great passing, had looked sharp in the win over Detroit. Wade, besides throwing for three touch-downs, had confused the Lion defense by alternating his snap count, drawing the Lions offsides three times. He was off to his best year as a professional quarterback.

The defense, although giving up a season-high twenty-one points against Detroit, still continued to force turnovers. Keyed by Richie Pe-titbon's interception for a touchdown against the Lions, the defense had now intercepted an amazing eleven passes through the first three games. Up front, Doug Atkins was causing opponents nightmares with his pass rush. Opposing quarterbacks were feeling the heat from the Bears' constant pressure and were being forced into making poor deci-sions. Safety Roosevelt Taylor, utilizing his tremendous speed, was leading the team in tackles. George Allen's simplified system was paying huge dividends in the early part of the season.

ROOSEVELT TAYLOR (Defensive Back): "George Allen worked twenty-four hours a day. George was like my college coach, Eddie Robinson—they could never get enough football, they just worked around the clock. He always had us prepared to play."

The 3–0 start was the best start for a Bears team since 1948, and a capacity crowd of more than forty-eight thousand fans turned out to witness the team's home opener. Most fans who expected to see an offensive explosion were surprised when neither team was able to score in the first thirty minutes of play.

The Colts struck first midway through the third quarter when Jim Martin's 16-yard field goal put Baltimore up 3–0. Halas, disappointed with his team's lack of offensive production, made a surprise move, replacing Bill Wade with Rudy Bukich. Wade, who had struggled all game long, was not aided by the play of his receivers, who dropped many passes. Bukich, seeing his first action of the season, moved the offense down the field, highlighted by a long pass to Mike Ditka. The drive stalled at the Colts' 28-yard line, where a Bob Jencks field-goal try went wide left. The Colts still led 3–0 as the third quarter came to a close.

On their next possession, the Bears again drove down the field on a series of short passes and the strong running of Joe Marconi and Ronnie Bull. After a holding penalty moved the ball back to the Colts' 44-yard line, Bukich faked a dive to Marconi, then hit Bull at the 40-yard line with a short pass. Bull broke to his right, picked up a crushing block by Mike Ditka on the Colts' Bobby Boyd, and ran untouched into the end zone for the touchdown. Jencks added the extra point.

Baltimore, now trailing 7–3, turned the ball over on their first play from scrimmage. Unitas, attempting to pass, was hit hard by Stan Jones and fumbled. Bears defensive end Bob Kilcullen dove on the loose ball at the Colts' 22-yard line. Four plays later, Roger LeClerc's 16-yard field goal gave the Bears a 10–3 lead.

The Colts tried again to rally behind Unitas, but the Bears' defense, led by the front four of Doug Atkins, Earl Leggett, Stan Jones, and Bob Kilcullen, sacked Unitas twice. The Bears prevailed 10–3 to push their unbeaten record to 4–0.

Halas was in a giddy mood following his team's fourth straight victory of the season. The old man knew his team had dodged a bullet. The defense was again outstanding, and the offense, ignited by Rudy Bukich's fine play, scored when they needed to. Halas talked about the scoring play, the pass to Ronnie Bull in the fourth quarter. "We had used it before . . . on the second play of the game, but Ditka dropped the pass. We talked about it between halves, but I didn't send it in. Rudy called it himself." The play was designed to flood the left side of the field with receivers. This allowed Bull to cut through the line, then break out to the right side of the field unnoticed. Thanks to Ditka's thunderous block on Boyd, Bull had an easy run to pay dirt.

John Unitas, in the quiet Colts locker room, was complimentary of the Bears' defense, especially the front four. "I thought the Bears defense played as well as I have seen them play in a long time. They are always tough to play against, but their pass rush today was fierce. We just couldn't get into our rhythm, mainly because of those guys up front. They were tough today." The Colts, now 1–3, would go home to face San Francisco, the only team that they had defeated this year. The Bears would go back on the road to face the Rams in Los Angeles.

ROGER LECLERC (Kicker): "We were warming up before the game, and Halas is talking to us. He said, 'Men, there is only one reason we will lose this game . . . one reason only. Does anybody know what that reason is?' I yelled out, 'Complacency!' Halas says, 'Who said that?' I'm thinking he's mad, so I quickly yell back, 'Bennie McRae.' He walks over to McRae and gives him a hundred dollars. McRae later wouldn't split it with me."

DAN SULLIVAN (Offensive Tackle, Baltimore Colts): "Johnny Unitas—in all the years I played with John, he would never get on a lineman for a physical mistake. If you were having a problem blocking someone, he would come over to you on the sideline and say, 'You having a tough day with so-and-so? How can I help you? What do you need? You want to set him up for a trap, to slow him down a little bit.' He would never get on you for physical mistakes, but if you made a mental mistake he would rip you up one side and down the other. But he was supremely confident, cocksure of himself. He felt he could always bring the team back and win the football game."

MAURY YOUMANS (Defensive End): "We all used to like to get Doug Atkins fired up for the Colts and their great offensive lineman, Jim Parker. Those two were probably two of the greatest players to ever play the game. We would work on Doug and tell him Parker said he was going to 'kick his ass' on Sunday. Doug wouldn't say anything, but you could tell he was getting ready for Parker. Those two would go at it, calling each other every name you could think of. They would just beat each other up the whole game. Those two were the real deal."

JOHNNY UNITAS (Quarterback, Baltimore Colts): "One of Doug Atkins's favorite tricks was to throw a blocker at the quarterback. The man had amazing strength."

Ed O'BRADOVICH

DEFENSIVE END

The fact that we played with a veteran team, guys that were playing eight, ten, twelve years in the league, made a difference. They set the tone, and if somebody on the opposition tried something, they got taken care of.

"One night I came back half-stiff, and Doug Atkins was in the room playing darts. I wanted to play darts with him, but he wouldn't let me. I grabbed the darts from him, and he picked me up and dropped me like a sack of potatoes.

"Bill George and I became the best of friends. The day that he got killed, he was going out to this industrial plant near Rockford to pick up some industrial filters he had ordered. They had drop-shipped them by mistake to this company. He picked up the order and was driving back to where his warehouse was. He got whacked by an eighteen-wheeler at an intersection. He made a trip that in reality he didn't have to make, but that was Bill George. He played fifteen years in the NFL. That was Bill taking care of business."

Ed O'Bradovich. Courtesy of Chicago Bears.

1963 version of the Bears' Kingston trio. *Left to right:* Bob Wetoska, Dave Whitsell, and Maury Youmans. Courtesy of Maury Youmans.

10

Locker Room Stories

MIKE DITKA (Tight End): "People in the league today don't understand that the game of football is a thing that is going to go on and on. They forget who started the f--king game, who took care of it, who made the game what it is. We all are caretakers of the game, but these people today don't understand that. They think they are the game now. They are a very small part of the game. They are going to be here and then gone. They just happened to be in the game at the right time when they were making all the money, that's all. I am sure George Halas is doing flip-flops in his grave because of what the hell is going on in the League and how much money they are paying these people. Things like that would drive any sane man nuts."

ROGER DAVIS (Offensive Guard): "We had a poker game that was ongoing during training camp. You had to bolt your food down to get to the game. Same guys played all the time: Bill George, Rick Casares, Mike Ditka, Richie Petibone. . . . Then after the season started we would play once a week in this guy's apartment. Johnny Morris used to play all the time. One game we played, all the cards were down, you couldn't see the other people's cards, high-low. In this one particular game we were splitting the pot. Half the pot went to the high spade, the other half went to the best hand. I had the ace of spades right off, and Ditka had three of a kind. On the fifth card he hit four treys. So I would raise, he would raise back. Because I had the high spade I already was guaranteed half the pot. To make a long story short, the last card I catch was the jack of spades, for a royal flush. When it came time to turn the cards over, me being a smart-ass, I showed the ten of spades because I had all the rest of them. He looked at me like something was wrong, and then I showed the rest of them. Ditka threw the cards in my face—he was furious. He hated to lose at anything—cards, tiddlywinks, or anything else."

MAURY YOUMANS (Defensive End): "Johnny Morris used to play gin rummy all the time with Angie Coia. One day Angie asked me to let him have that marked deck I used in my magic tricks. We were going on a trip, and Johnny and Angie used to play gin rummy on the plane. So when we we're getting off the plane, I asked Angie, 'How did the marked deck work?' Angie says, 'Well, the only thing I could see was the winning card for him before it came up.' I think Johnny was one of the luckiest guys going."

ROGER DAVIS (Offensive Guard): "One time during the exhibition season we were on the road, and a bunch of us told Doug Atkins that Stan Fanning could outeat and outdrink him. Fanning we called Superman, because he could eat and drink so much. So Doug and Stan go out for a martini contest. I think Stan drank like twenty-one and Doug drank twenty-three. I believe Doug drank two more just to show there was no question who won. Then they have to go back for a team meeting. Well, we hide Stan in the back, but you could not hide Doug when he had a few too many. He was in the front row, protesting everything said. I remember Halas was going through a kickoff play. Halas says, 'Any questions?' Doug shouts out, 'How long has it been since you ran down under a kickoff, old man?' You could have heard a pin drop. Halas says, 'All right, Doug, everybody knows you're here.' Those two didn't get along, but the old man loved him."

MAURY YOUMANS (Defensive End): "Angie Coia and I were going to the track, and Johnny Morris asked me to bet on a horse for him, but he didn't give me any money. We get back and I had forgot about it, and the horse won. Richie Petibone says, 'Well, you got to pay him.' Johnny says, 'Instead of paying me, I'll cut cards with you.' So we cut cards three or four times, and I lost every time. Now I'm triple the money I owed him. What saved me here was we were going out to San Francisco to play, and Angie had this guy he knew out there that was a great handicapper. We meet at the track and proceed to win every race but the second, which we lost by a nose. I took that money and gave it to Johnny. I was so thankful just to get him off my back."

ROGER DAVIS (Offensive Guard): "One year Halas had the Burns Detective Agency following us. He went into his speech about certain places he didn't want us to go, and we weren't supposed to drink, and he didn't want us in those bars. He ended up by saying, 'You c--ksuckers who drink at home, there's no hope for you anyway.' He could be brutal at times."

CHUCK MATHER (Coach): "Doug would give Halas a hard time. He'd be out and have too much to drink and call Halas up at 2:00 A.M. and tell him, 'Halas, what a f--king coach you are.' Halas was about the only coach who could put up with him. Paul Brown couldn't handle him. On Sundays Doug was a great player, which is what counts in pro ball."

ROGER DAVIS (Offensive Guard): "When Bill George played cards and he was doing badly, he would get mad. He'd deal opposite the way you were supposed to. Nobody ever dared say anything to him."

STAN JONES (Defensive Tackle): "Somebody was playing their music too loud during training camp one year. Doug had this pistol and he shot it off, right up through the floor. We never had anybody playing music after hours again."

RICK CASARES (Fullback): "Bobby Layne and I got to be real close friends out in the Pro Bowl and later in Vegas. One Sunday we're playing the Lions, and I go running by him, warming up before the game. The night before the Detroit games, I would tell the hotel switchboard not to put any calls through, unless it was George Halas. I knew Bobby would be calling me to go out, and I never went out the night before a game. You could put a gun to my head, I still wouldn't go out. Anyway, I run by Bobby and he says in that whiskey voice of his, 'God damn, Rick, where were you last night? I was at the Playboy Club until 2:00 A.M. Where were you?' I told him I must have just missed him. There was no way I would go out, but I wouldn't tell Bobby that. The next day he throws three touchdown passes. Bobby was amazing."

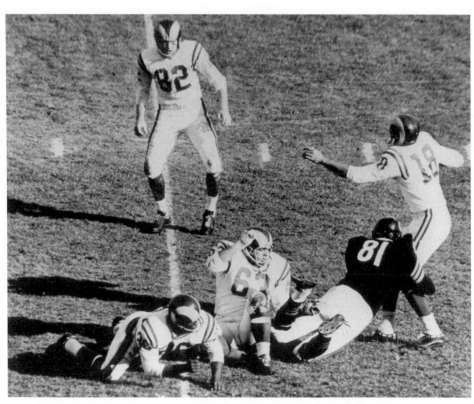

Doug Atkins harasses the Rams' Roman Gabriel. Courtesy of Doug Atkins.

11

Los Angeles Rams

The Bears headed to the West Coast to play the winless Los Angeles Rams on Sunday, followed by a game a week later in San Francisco, against the 49ers. Still perfect after four games, Halas was hounded by the media regarding his thoughts on his team going all the way this year. The old coach continued to insist it was way too early to predict anything. On paper this week's game against the Rams looked like a mismatch, but Papa Bear had seen this type of game before. "In the NFL you have to be ready to play every week," Halas said. "Or your going to get beat, it happens all the time. Believe me, we will have our hands full on Sunday with the Rams. Don't let their record fool you, they're a much better team than that. We have had some tough games out there over the years and I don't expect this to be any different." Halas hoped the players felt the same way.

The Green Bay Packers, after their opening game loss to the Bears, had reeled off three straight wins, soundly beating Detroit 31–10, Baltimore 31–20, and the Rams 42–10. Coach Vince Lombardi made it clear in his weekly meeting with the press that the Bears were not the only strong team in the Western Conference. "If anyone thinks the Green Bay Packers are on a decline just because we lost one game this year, forget it. This 1963 team is the best group I have had since I have been in Green Bay," said a feisty Lombardi. Green Bay's head coach felt that competition in the Western Conference was so strong that certainly no team would go undefeated, and probably a 10–4 record would be good enough to win the Western crown. Lombardi then added, "The season still has a long way to go, of course with each game it gets shorter and shorter and increases the chances of a better than 10–4 record taking it." He went on to talk about the emergence of Minnesota as a contender, making the competition stiffer each week for his team. "We've got more traditional rivals than any other team. The Bears, the Lions and now the Vikings," Lombardi said. "I don't like it. It gets those boys all the more aroused when they play us. But there is only one way to play this game. You win what you can win and you hate like hell to lose the ones you have to lose. If you don't feel that way, you might as well quit." The bottom line on all of this was that Lombardi felt the Western Conference race was still wide open. His team was healthy and playing well. He knew down the line his Packers would have another crack at the upstart Bears.

Quarterback Bill Wade was looking forward to playing his old team, the Rams. "I think there's always a little more motivation when you go up against your old team, but my focus this week, like every week, is to play well and help my team win." Wade had been acquired in 1961 as part of a complex trade among the Bears, Giants, and Rams. The Rams received Zeke Bratkowski and Erich Barnes for Wade and a draft pick. The Rams then traded Barnes and linebacker John Guzig to the Giants for defensive back Lindon Crow. The Rams used their picks in 1962 to select Roman Gabriel and Merlin Olsen. It had been a trade that was good for all the teams involved, but unfortunately for the Rams, their record the past few years didn't indicate that. In 1962, head coach Bob Waterfield had been fired after eight games with a record of 1–7–0. Waterfield was replaced by Harland Svare, but the change in coaches didn't help as the Rams finished the year 0–5–1. Losing their first four games of 1963 put Svare's coaching record at 0–9–1. The young coach was starting to feel the heat from the media and fans alike. "I would be the first to say that we are a much better team than our record indicates," said a cautious Svare. "Injuries have slowed our progress down, but we are getting better. People have to be patient as it takes time to build a strong team in the NFL. We are looking forward to playing the Bears, they are a very good team." When asked why George Halas seemed to be the only NFL coach who could roam the sidelines freely, never restricted to staying between the 40-yard line hash marks, Svare answered. "Well he's an old man, I suppose the officials have to cater to his whims." Anyone, but especially a rival coach, who dared suggest that George Halas was given special advantages was not looked fondly upon by Papa Bear. Although he had no comment for that remark, Halas's interviews leading up to the game became short and to the point. It was clear, George Halas would let his team do the talking for him on Sunday.

The Bears' defensive coordinator, George Allen, because of all the injuries, was forced to juggle his defensive lineup each week. Oddly, each time he was faced with replacing an injured player with a backup, the defense played better. Stan Jones, Bob Kilcullen and John Johnson had been offensive linemen, converted over to the defense, who had provided solid play along the front wall.

Defensive assistant Joe Stydahar also had ties to Los Angeles. He had coached the Rams in the early 1950s, winning the 1951 NFL Championship over the Cleveland Browns, 24–17. Strangely, the next season Stydahar decided to resign after one game. In 1953 he was hired by the Chicago Cardinals, but lasted only two seasons, finishing with an abysmal 3–20–1 record. He believed in hard work, and the Bears' front line was playing well under him. When asked why he thought the defense was so much improved this year, he offered these insights: "We work each week on fundamentals. Our philosophy is to pursue on every play. The chase, so to speak, with the use of speed and mobility to keep constant pressure on the opposition."

The Bears' offense had scored fourteen times so far this season, twelve of those chances set up by the defense. For the year, George Allen's crew had given up a total of 34 points, 52 points fewer than a year ago.

All systems were go on October 13, 1963, as the Bears took the field at the L.A. Coliseum to play the Los Angeles Rams. If George Halas had revenge on his mind for Harland Svare's ill-timed comments about him, his team didn't disappoint him with their play. The Bears, displaying no signs of overconfidence, totally destroyed the Rams that day in every possible way. When the carnage was over, the Bears had delivered the worst beating ever afflicted on a Rams team, 52–14. Each aspect of Chicago's powerful team came into play. The offense picked up 22 first downs, rushing for 85 yards on the ground, while adding another 201 yards through the air. Sharing the quarterback position, Bill Wade and Rudy Bukich each had performed well. Wade completed 12 of 21 passes, for 3 touchdowns, while Bukich, in a mop-up role, completed 8 of 9 passes, for 2 touchdowns. Tight end Mike Ditka caught 9 passes for 110 yards, 4 of which went for touchdowns, which tied a Bears record. Three of Ditka's touchdowns came from Wade, with the fourth from Bukich.

The defense intercepted 6 passes, for an amazing 126 yards in returns. This was just 11 yards less than the Rams' total passing yardage for the game. Included in the six interceptions was a nifty 35-yard return for a touchdown by cornerback Bennie McRae. This defensive gem came just fifty-five seconds after Ditka had scored the game's first touchdown. The Rams never recovered from the two quick scores.

The hapless Los Angeles Rams, in losing their ninth straight game over two seasons, had turned the ball over eight times during the game. Keeping the press waiting for thirty minutes following the lopsided affair, Halas offered this about his 5–0 team: "This isn't a great team but it's a helluva good one. That Bill Wade to Mike Ditka combination, is one of the best I have ever had. Make no mistake, we were hot, especially when Wade and Bukich are hitting like that, there just isn't a defense to stop them. Bukich did every bit as good today, as he did in pulling us out last Sunday against Baltimore. We have two very good quarterbacks on this team."

Former Bears quarterback Zeke Bratkowski had suffered through a horrible afternoon as the Rams' signal caller. Under constant pressure from the Bears' defense, Bratkowski had his worst afternoon as an NFL quarterback. "This was as bad as it gets," he said in the Rams' locker room following the game. "We knew going into the game how good this Bears defense was, but I didn't expect this. We just couldn't get anything going today. They have a great defense, easily the best we have seen this year. They are relentless."

The team would stay on the West Coast, traveling up to Sonoma, in the Valley of the Moon, to prepare for the San Francisco 49ers next week at Kezar Stadium. Once again they would play a team looking for its first victory of the season.

ROGER LECLERC (Kicker): "I was originally brought in to be a linebacker to eventually replace Bill George, but I did some kicking on the side, which Halas liked. The more he could get out of you, the better he liked it. Every year I won the kicking job by default. They drafted Bob Jencks as a kicker, and we split the kicking duties. He did the points after, and I did the field goals. He had the whole job in 1963 but had problems, so Halas told me to do the field goals. Neither of us liked the situation, but that's what Halas wanted."

BILL WADE (Quarterback): "I had respect for 90 percent of the guys in the locker room. There were only one or two that I didn't think should have been there, but it wasn't up to me to say. I felt all the guys had their own way of thinking. I never thought of them being in a religious mode. I was hoping on Sunday they'd be in a fighting mode. They usually were. There were a lot of rough guys in that locker room, and I expected that. To me, my faith was kind of a personal challenge to maintain those feelings and not be ashamed of them. My spiritual aspect was, 'Hey, look, you believe in God? He hasn't disappeared.' Either it meant something to you or it didn't mean something to you. Well, it meant something to me. It is a very serious matter which I felt no human could destroy, although there were humans who tried to destroy it. I said, 'I'll leave this up to God and let me see what he is going to do with this guy, or that one, or whatever.' "

Mr. Bear, Rick Casares. Courtesy of Rick Casares.

12

San Francisco 49ers

The Bears with their convincing win over the Rams remained in first place in the Western Conference, with a perfect 5–0 record. Green Bay, in beating Minnesota 37–28, improved their record to 4–1, but still trailed the Bears by one game. The Vikings, Detroit, and Baltimore at 2–3 were all tied for third place in the West. San Francisco and Los Angeles both were still looking for their first victories of the season.

In the Eastern Conference, the Cleveland Browns, after defeating the New York Giants 35–24, were in first place at 5–0. The Giants, the preseason pick to return to the championship game, now at 3–2, fell two games behind the Browns in the race for the top spot. The St. Louis Cardinals, with only one loss, were in second place, one game behind Cleveland. The Cardinals would face Green Bay at home on Sunday.

Halas again tried to downplay the Bears' complete destruction of the Los Angeles Rams. "We are playing way over our heads, but I'm keeping my fingers crossed," the Bears' head coach told the press. "It's wonderful to have a one-two punch at quarterback, with Bill Wade and Rudy Bukich." Halas also praised his tight end Mike Ditka. "He is becoming one of the fine players in this league. He took his eyes off the first one Wade threw, but there was nothing wrong with him the rest of the way." Ditka, with four touchdowns against the Rams, was currently leading the NFL in touchdown receptions, with seven.

Chicago's head coach did voice some concerns about veteran running back Willie Galimore, who fumbled twice against the Rams. "We have brought Willie along slowly," said a disappointed Halas. "He needs to take better care of the ball. He's a little rusty, from lack of playing, but hopefully that touchdown he got against the Rams will get him going. After two knee operations, many players would not even be on the squad." Galimore had one of his finest games against the 49ers last year, gaining 181 yards and scoring two touchdowns. Halas was contemplating starting Galimore on Sunday against the 49ers.

The team would spend five days in Sonoma, fifty miles northwest of San Francisco, practicing at a high school complex. Halas decided to work his team in seclusion, away from the bright lights of the Bay Area and all the temptations it offered. The players still figured out ways to entertain themselves.

BOB WETOSKA (Offensive Lineman): "Doug Atkins and Fred Williams decided to have this drinking contest when we were out on the West Coast. They drank an amazing amount of martinis between them. When they staggered back to the hotel, Freddy passes out in the elevator. Doug, instead of picking him up, just grabs him by his ankles and pulls him down the hallway to his room. Freddy the next morning has all these rug burns on his back and elbows, from being dragged across the floor. When someone asked him about who won the drinking contest, he says, 'Well, Doug must have won, because he had to drag me home.' "

The San Francisco 49ers had fired their head coach, Red Hickey, after three games in 1963, replacing him with assistant coach, Jack Christiansen. The 49ers then proceeded to drop two more games under Christiansen, which extended their two-year losing streak to seven games. The 49ers had lost starting quarterback John Brodie before the season because of an automobile accident. Holdover Bobby Waters and recently acquired Lamar McHan had been ineffective in last week's 20–3 loss to the Colts. The San Francisco defense, ranked next to last in points allowed, needed to be rebuilt. Longtime players Leo Nomellini, Charlie Kreuger, and Matt Hazeltine were showing rapid decline in play. On offense the 49ers were respectable, with a core of solid players. Running back J. D. Smith, wide receiver Bernie Casey, and tight end Monty Stickles were all proven players, but the lack of depth in the offensive line hurt the team's progress. Only tackle Bob St. Clair was All-Pro caliber. The 49er fans, becoming accustomed to inept play by their team, now took to ridiculing them. An apathetic crowd of only 32,000 was expected for the game on Sunday.

Kezar Stadium, home to the 49ers since 1946, was built in 1922 through the generous donation of Mary A. Kezar. A longtime Bay Area resident, Kezar contributed $100,000 to the building of the stadium as a memorial to her departed mother and relatives. The San Francisco Parks and Recreation Department then appropriated another $200,000 toward its completion. The one-tier stadium, with a capacity of 59,942, over the years had developed a reputation as a tough place to perform, especially for kickers. The wind blowing off the bay could change in the blink of an eye, which made kicking at times almost impossible. The coin flip took on a whole new meaning at Kezar Stadium.

The Bears entered the game as a solid nineteen-point favorite. Halas, unhappy with his team's efforts at practice during the week, lamented his concerns to the media. "There seems to be a complacency that I didn't like in practice," he told the writers on Thursday. "The only way we can lose to the 49ers Sunday, is to enter the game flat and complacent."

Besides the apparent lack of concentration, the weather didn't help the Bears' practices either, as it rained most of the week, turning the practice field into a sea of mud. The Bears headed for San Francisco on Saturday with a very concerned head coach.

San Francisco won the toss and elected to receive. Behind the strong play of quarterback Lamar McHan, the 49ers looked far from a team sporting a 0–5 record. McHan, smartly mixing in a series of short passes along with the strong running of J. D. Smith, marched his team down the field. On the ninth play of the drive, fullback Jim Vollenweider plunged over from the 1-yard line for the score. Kicker Tommy Davis added the extra point, giving San Francisco an early 7–0 lead.

The two teams continued to exchange possessions before Davis late in the first quarter kicked a 25-yard field goal to stretch the 49ers' lead to 10–0.

The Bears back on offense were still unable to move the ball and were again forced to punt. The 49ers, becoming more confident on each play, moved the ball to their own 44-yard line, setting up a critical third-down play. McHan, forced out of the pocket by Earl Leggett, moved to his right where he spotted tight end Don Lisbon open at the Bears' 15-yard line. McHan released the ball as Stan Jones hit him, knocking him to the ground. Lisbon, breaking toward the outside, caught the ball over the outstretched hand of Bears defender Dave Whitsell, falling forward to the Bears' 7-yard line. Underdog San Francisco, ahead 10–0, had a first and goal deep in Bears territory. McHan on first down rolled out to the right where he found Gary Knafelc open in the end zone for the touchdown. Davis's kick extended San Francisco's lead to 17–0.

Chicago, with only a few minutes to go in the first half, finally began to move the football. Quarterback Bill Wade completed three straight passes to move the Bears into 49ers territory. On a second and eight from the 49ers' 43-yard line, Wade found Johnny Morris deep across the middle for a beautiful 38-yard completion, giving the Bears a first down inside the 49ers' 5-yard line. After a Rick Casares dive, plus a 49ers offside penalty that moved the ball to the 1-yard line, Wade hit John Farrington across the middle for the touchdown. Bob Jencks's extra point pulled the Bears within ten points as the teams headed for the dressing rooms.

San Francisco midway through the third quarter extended its lead to 20–7 on Tommy Davis's 45-yard field goal. George Halas, with his team struggling to make a first down, inserted Rudy Bukich into the lineup for Wade. Bukich completed four straight passes, which moved the Bears near the 49er goal line as the third quarter came to a close. Early in the fourth quarter the Bears scored, as Bukich dove over for a touchdown. Jencks's point after cut the 49ers' lead to 20–14.

The Bears, now within striking distance of the 49ers, made numerous mistakes that halted drives. First, reliable Mike Ditka dropped a certain third-down catch at midfield, ending a Chicago possession. Then in the next series, Johnny Morris was five yards behind the 49ers' secondary, but Bukich's pass was overthrown. Late in the game Kermit Alexander correctly timed a Bukich pass intended for Morris to make an interception, stopping another drive. Finally with just over a minute to go, the Bears had one last chance. On first down Bukich hit Morris on a sideline pattern for 17 yards. On the next play 49ers linebacker Ed Pine intercepted another Bukich pass, this one in the flat to seal the Bears' fate. Upstart San Francisco had beaten the Bears 20–14 in the biggest upset of the year in the NFL.

George Halas in the locker room had nothing but kind words for the victors. "This was an aroused team and they took every advantage of every opportunity. This team was poised to upset somebody and that somebody was the Chicago Bears."

The Bears had turned the ball over four times on three interceptions and one fumble. The Bears' defense, leaders so far this season in take-aways, had only one turnover for the game. Two apparent Richie Petitbon interceptions were reversed by the officials, one being overruled as a trapped ball, the other lost because of pass interference. Although Halas vehemently argued both the trapped ball and the pass interference, he used neither as an excuse as to why his team had lost the game. The old man had warned of the possibility of an upset all week, so he was going to let it go. The players knew they had played poorly, but they never quit. It was time to go home and face the Philadelphia Eagles. It was time to get back down to business.

RICHIE PETITBON (Defensive Back): "Halas in a meeting following a loss asked if anybody had read the book *The Scarlet Letter*. One player raised his hand and said he had. Halas said, 'What was that about?' The player answered it was about a woman who committed adultery, and she had to wear an *A* on her breast. Halas said, 'That's right, and just like this last ball game, like her, we got f--ked.' "

Rick CASARES

FULLBACK

eorge Halas was always telling me to go out with the right girls. I started dating a girl by the name of Suzy Smith who was the niece of the county commissioner. There happened to be a mention of this in one of the newspaper columns one morning. Anyway, I go to practice, and Halas calls me over and says, 'Rick, I'm glad to see you finally going out with a nice girl, rather than those racetrack floozies.'

"Now it's Thanksgiving, and I was invited to Suzy's parents' home. I go to their condominium and spend the whole afternoon there and had a nice time. I had planned on the way home to stop at this friend of mine's bar, to wish his mother a happy birthday. He had asked me to please stop as he knew it would mean a lot to his mother, so I did. I walk in and we sit down at the bar. They were opening some champagne and I was turned, talking to Suzy, when I felt somebody sit down next to me. I turn around and it's George Halas, in a black hat and a black coat. I said, 'Hi, Coach.' He says, 'Rick, I'm really disappointed in you. You have been shacked up all afternoon, and now you are down here drinking and we got a big game coming up on Sunday. The team's counting on you, and you're in a bar drinking.' Suzy's on my right, hearing all this. I'm thinking to myself, 'Now I got my

Rick Casares. Courtesy of Chicago Bears.

chance,' so I said to him, 'Coach, I want to introduce you to someone
I've been shacked up with all afternoon. Coach, I want to introduce
you to Suzy Smith. Suzy, this is George Halas.' Suzy said, 'Mr. Halas,
Rick was having dinner with my parents and myself all afternoon at our
apartment.' Halas for the first time, probably in his life, didn't know
what to say. He had me followed. He was coming down there to lower
the boom on me. He just got up and left and never mentioned it
again."

Johnny Morris catches another pass against the Eagles. Courtesy of Chicago Bears.

13

Philadelphia Eagles

The Chicago Bears and the Philadelphia Eagles began playing back in 1935. Prior to 1963 the Bears had won twelve of the fourteen games played, with one contest ending in a tie. Their last meeting between these old rivals, in 1961, had a bizarre ending. Trailing by two points in the fourth quarter, Roger LeClerc missed an easy field goal, preventing the Bears from taking the lead. Later in the game the Bears again were in easy field-goal range, but for some unexplained reason Bill George lined up and kicked the ball instead of LeClerc. The attempt sailed wide left, and the Bears lost the game, 16–14. No explanation was ever given by anyone why George kicked instead of LeClerc.

The Philadelphia Eagles began play in 1933 when Bert Bell and his partner, Lud Wray, purchased the Frankford, Pennsylvania, Yellow Jackets, and relocated the team to Philadelphia. The partners decided to give the team the nickname Eagles, after the symbol of the National Recovery Administration, which had been created as part of President Franklin Roosevelt's New Deal program.

Bert Bell, born De Benneville Bell on February 25, 1894, was raised in an upper-middle-class home, just outside of Philadelphia. His father, Upton Bell, served as attorney general of Pennsylvania, and his brother later went on to become governor. Young Bert, who had no interest in politics, loved sports, especially football. A superb athlete, Bell went to the University of Pennsylvania, where he became the starting quarterback in 1916. Besides being the quarterback on the Quakers' football team, he served as the punter and place kicker and was the team's best defender. Following the 1916 season, Penn was selected to play in the Rose Bowl against Oregon. In a hard-fought game, Penn lost to the Ducks 14–0, but Bert Bell made history that day. He was credited with throwing the first forward pass in Rose Bowl history.

With his country now deep into the Great War, Bert Bell decided to forego his senior year and enlisted in the army. Stationed in France, he was assigned to the general field hospital where he remained throughout the war. Following his discharge from the army, he returned to Penn for one final season. Upon graduation, he was asked by Coach John Heisman to stay on as assistant football coach. He coached at Penn for nine years.

In 1933 Bell, along with a former Quaker teammate, decided to buy a professional football team. Because he lacked his share of the money needed, he turned to his father for a loan. His father flatly turned him down. His explanation was quick and to the point: "My son, in high society, college football is the thing to do, but to spend your money on professional football, something that will never make it, is foolish. I will not lend you a nickel for such a folly." Desperate, Bert turned to his mother who, against her husband's opposition, loaned him his share of the money needed to purchase the Frankford Yellow Jackets.

In the early years Bell served as president, coach, business manager, publicist, and ticket manager. He worked eighteen hours a day to make the Eagles a success. While the Eagles were never a strong team on the field those first few years, Bell's passion for the game provided great leadership for his team and his league. Later he would sell his interest in the Eagles and become part owner of the Pittsburgh Steelers. Chosen commissioner of the league in 1946, he oversaw the NFL absorbing the All-American Conference's top three teams, the Cleveland Browns, the Baltimore Colts, and the San Francisco 49ers. Bert Bell died on a Sunday afternoon in 1959, watching the Philadelphia Eagles play football. Like his counterpart in Chicago, George Halas, Bell was a true legend of the game.

The Philadelphia Eagles, entering their seventh game of the 1963 season, against the Bears, had a record of 2–3–1. The previous Sunday the Eagles had lost to the Cleveland Browns, 37–7. In that game starting quarterback Sonny Jurgensen had suffered a bone-chip fracture, severely bruised his right shoulder, and was probably lost for the year. Also injured in the Browns game were star receiver Tommy McDonald, who had suffered a slight shoulder separation, and star linebacker Maxie Baughn, who had broken his thumb. Both players' availability for the Chicago game was doubtful.

The Eagles, who had won the NFL crown in 1960, were in a rebuilding process in 1963. Gone were legendary players Norm Van Brocklin, Tom Brookshier, and Chuck Bednarik. The Eagles' head coach, Buck Shaw, had retired following the 1960 season and was replaced by Nick Skorich, now in his third year. Skorich had the challenge of trying to rebuild the Eagles into a contender in the Eastern Conference. First on his list was to improve a very poor defensive team. The offense was very good, but the defense, through six games, was near the bottom of the league in points allowed. Skorich knew it was impossible to win consistently in the NFL with such a lousy defense. Young players like Maxie Baughn, Irv Cross, and LeRoy Caffey were a solid nucleus to build around.

On offense, the veteran Jurgensen was considered to be one of the best quarterbacks in the game. Throwing for twenty-two touchdowns last season, Jurgensen was again on track for another terrific year before his injury. Although backup King Hill had seen little action this season, he had played previously with the St. Louis Cardinals. Hill was hoping for a big game in his surprise start against the Bears on Sunday. The Bears respected Hill as a quarterback but were more concerned with his outstanding trio of receivers, which included the elusive McDonald, tight end Pete Retzlaff, and halfback Tim Brown. All three men were above-average football players. The Eagles' ground game with Brown, Ted Dean, and Clarence Peeke was improving. The Bears' defense would be challenged by this very good offensive team.

The Bears, following their upset lost to the 49ers, returned to Chicago in a foul mood. Players and coaches alike knew they had given one away and were now tied with Green Bay for first place in the West, each with 5–1 records. While Chicago was being upset by San Francisco, the Packers had destroyed the St. Louis Cardinals, 30–7. In winning the game, the Packers like the Eagles had lost their starting quarterback to injury. Bart Starr, hit out-of-bounds by St. Louis defender Jimmy Hill, slugged Hill in the helmet with his right arm, breaking his wrist. His status on when he would return to the Green Bay lineup was uncertain. Cardinal coach Wally Lemm, in defending his player's questionable tactics, referred to Packer fullback Jim Taylor as a dirty player. Vince Lombardi, on hearing Lemm's bashing of Taylor, went ballistic. "If he called Taylor a dirty football player, then he's an unstable man, running off at the mouth . . . and make sure you use the word *if*," an angry Lombardi told the St. Louis press. Clearly, behind the war of words was the concern that the Packer offense would now be without Bart Starr for an extended period of time. John Roach, a little-used backup, would get his first NFL start Sunday against the Baltimore Colts.

Coach Halas used the loss to San Francisco as a reminder to his team of how competitive the NFL was week in and week out. "We will play them one game at a time. We were flat and they were aroused. Such a set of circumstances invariably produces an unexpected result," he explained. "The 49ers were being ridiculed by the press and that just aroused them. Our players understand now that the 'important game,' is the next game, not one down the road. You can't look ahead in this league and be successful. We respect every team in the league," Halas added.

The players for their part decided to have a team meeting and clear the air. The season had been magical with five straight wins to start the season. The four team captains didn't want one loss to be a cause for finger-pointing. "It's a chance to get ourselves all braced again and start fresh. If anybody has anything to say, let them cut loose," said center Mike Pyle. "We all let off some steam, just what we needed to get ready for the Eagles on Sunday," Pyle remarked following the meeting.

George Halas had seen many "players only" meetings and admitted they have their place during the long season. "This thing has been going on for twenty years. Teams will have four or five such meetings a year. I encourage them." The players as a whole vowed to be better prepared come Sunday against the Eagles. "This team's got more pride than the other two Bears teams I have been on," Mike Ditka told the writers. "It's not a great ball club; but I don't think there's a great ball club in the league. But we're good enough to win the title."

Forty-eight thousand fans filled Wrigley Field on October 27, 1963, to watch the Eagles and Bears do battle. The Bears, a thirteen-point favorite at game time, came out fired up. The offense, behind quarterback Bill Wade and the hard running of fullback Joe Marconi, moved steadily down the field. After a penalty negated a Wade completion to Bull, Roger LeClerc kicked a 45-yard field goal to give the home team the early 3–0 lead. Chicago's defense, playing with much more intensity than a week before, shut the Eagles down on three straight running plays, stopping Ted Dean just inches short of a first down and forcing Philadelphia to punt. Returning to the field, the Bears' offense began their second drive from their own 33-yard line. After Ronnie Bull gained 2 yards off-tackle, Wade found Marconi open for a 22-yard gain and a first down at the Eagles' 43-yard line. Three running plays netted 20 yards, and the ball now rested on the Eagles' 23-yard line.

The Eagles' defense, having trouble with the Bears' ground game, began to move their defensive backs closer to the line of scrimmage. Spotting this, Wade faked a dive play to Bull, then threw to Marconi in the flat, where he ran untouched into the end zone for the touchdown. Bob Jencks's extra point put the Bears up 10–0. There was 2:45 left in the first quarter.

Midway through the second quarter, the Eagles' offense began to have some success against the Bears' defense. Three straight completions to tight end Pete Retzlaff moved the ball just inside the Chicago 40-yard line. After Tim Brown gained 7 yards off-tackle, Hill completed a 22-yard pass to rookie receiver Ron Goodwin for an Eagle first down inside the Bears' 10-yard line. Hill, again under pressure from the Bears' front line, rolled to his right and hit Tommy McDonald in the back of the end zone for the touchdown. Mike Clark's extra point cut the Bears' lead to 10–7. The first half ended with no further scoring.

The Bears' offense once again dominated play in the third period, as the Bears went on a seventeen-play drive that ate up most of the third period. Wade, again mixing short passes with the strong running of Marconi and Willie Galimore, moved the Bears' offense methodically down the field. At the Eagles' 7-yard line, Wade handed off to Galimore. Breaking through the line, Willie veered to his right, side-stepped Eagles defender Irv Cross, and sprinted into the end zone for the touchdown. Jencks missed his first extra point of the season, but the Bears increased their lead to 16–7.

Smelling victory, Chicago's defense took over the game. King Hill, under constant pressure, was knocked out late in the game by a vicious hit by Doug Atkins. Before being carried off, King had been intercepted three times in the fourth quarter. J. C. Caroline, Dave Whitsell, and Roosevelt Taylor each had a pick, as the Bears rolled to their sixth win of the year, 16–7.

In the relieved Bears' locker room, the players were happy to get a win, even though everyone felt the team could have played much better. "We were pretty sloppy," said a tired Mike Pyle. The Bears had dominated on offense, but a couple of costly mistakes and penalties had prevented the offense from scoring more points. Bill Wade, playing the entire game, completed 20 of 35 pass attempts, for 241 yards and a touchdown. Joe Marconi, subbing for the injured Rick Casares, gained 67 yards on 16 carries. He also caught 5 passes for an additional 69 yards and a touchdown. Willie Galimore also saw more action due to Ronnie Bull being kicked in the head in the second quarter. Galimore, in scoring another rushing touchdown, seemed to be gaining confidence each week. When he was right, he could make a defensive player look silly with his elusive moves. When "Willie the Wisp" was feeling good, he had few equals in the NFL.

During the press conference following the game, a writer asked George Halas, "How come the Bears didn't beat a lousy team like the Eagles worse?" Halas responded by saying, "First of all the Eagles are not a lousy team." The writer then pointed out that every team in the league scores 30 to 35 points against them. Halas again reiterated that the Eagles were not that bad. The writer, still not satisfied with Halas's answers, asked the old man if he had any good quotes. Halas replied, "No, and there won't be any!" Halas turned to his publicity man, Dan Demond, and said, "Dan, do you have a couple of good quotes for the boys?" Halas then walked out.

The Bears had done just enough to win. The players understood that at the end of the day, the only thing important was the win. The effort was there, the talent was in place, and next week in Baltimore they would find their rhythm. Baltimore's Memorial Stadium had been a good place for the Chicago Bears the past couple of years. They all looked forward to playing the Colts.

RICHIE PETITBON (Defensive Back): "All Doug Atkins ever wanted to do was rush the quarterback. I think they carried off nine quarterbacks one year. That's a pretty good year."

Papa Bear showing his displeasure on the Bears sideline. Courtesy of Chicago Bears.

14

Negotiating with Papa Bear; or, Anyone for a Root Canal?

Sitting down with George Halas to negotiate a contract was not a pleasant experience. In a time before sports agents, players were left to themselves to discuss contracts with the owner/coach. Rarely did a player get the best of him.

ED O'BRADOVICH (Defensive End): "The reality of it is that if it wasn't for the old man, there would be no National Football League . . . period. He was the guy that had the vision and the wherewithal to work it through. He gave to a lot of teams to keep them alive back in those old days. He always remembered those days, and that was probably why he was so tight. I am glad I played for the Bears . . . I'm proud to be a Chicago Bear . . . but the way things turned out money-wise, we sure got the low end of the stick."

MIKE PYLE (Center): "I can attest to the fact that George Halas always was thinking in terms of him getting paid back for the hard times he had making the NFL happen. I know that best from the first meeting we ever had with the owners and the player reps in 1966. I was the Bears' rep that year, and Ordelle Brasse was the players' union president. We had gotten the approval to have a meeting with the owners in 1965, so we met with them in January 1966. We all sat around this big table. We [the players] had no representation other than ourselves; we were not allowed to bring our counsel in. In that meeting Halas didn't say anything all day . . . always taking notes . . . taking notes. At the end he finally spoke and went through a long speech about what they went through to start the league, and his implication was, 'Why are you guys asking for all this? We should be able to get back what we lost in the early years.' I walked out of the room saying, 'Jesus Christ, don't ask me to pay for what happened to you in 1921. . . . The stands are full.' "

ROGER DAVIS (Offensive Guard): "When we were voting on the players' union, Halas said I got this oil well that will give you a better retirement than the union will. If you vote for the union, I'm going to take it away from you."

RICHIE PETITBON (Defensive Back): "He was a tough old guy to negotiate with. Ditka had it right when he said he threw nickels around like they were manhole covers—he was tough. I will say this to his credit: it was still the formative years for the NFL, so I don't think there was a lot of money back then."

STAN JONES (Defensive Tackle): "You would go in for a contract and it was always, 'Well, Stan, yes, you had a good year, but unfortunately the team had a bad year,' or vice versa. Another one was, 'I don't reward mediocrity.' I always loved that term. 'I can't justify that to the board of directors.' He was the board of directors."

ED O'BRADOVICH (Defensive End): "My relationship with Halas was one of love and hate. In the ten years that I was there, I held out four times trying to get more money. I lost all four times.

"I remember after we won that World Championship in 1963. I was on a two-year contract, and we got nothing from Halas for winning it. We got a paperweight from Mayor Daley. I remember Vince Lombardi gave the Green Bay players' wives mink jackets one year, a color TV the next. Carol Rosenblum matched the Colts' players' winning share, which I believe was six thousand dollars that year. We knew all this, and everybody's thinking what were we going to get because he hadn't won the championship in seventeen years. Halas is on his last legs, and you know, what better time for him to retire. We got nothing.

"The next year, now I'm thinking, 'Hey, I intercepted a pass that led to the winning touchdown,' so I felt I deserved more money. I waited one night for Halas to come out of the Purple Room. That was the coaches' room—they called it the Purple Room. That's where the coaches used to go and sit with Halas and drink after practices and games. I decided I'm going to wait for him.

"He comes out and I could see he had a few, so I figured now I got the old man. So I said, 'Coach, I'd like to talk to you.' Halas says, 'Sure, kid, come on in.' . . . So I walked into his room, and we sit down. I said, 'Coach, I want a five thousand dollar raise and an unlimited two-year contract.' . . . He says, 'No!' . . . I said, 'Let me try to finish here,' and he said, 'No! . . . You get nothing.' I said, 'Coach, come on, I had a hell of a year last year, we won the World Championship.' . . . He said, 'No!' . . . He just stared at me, and I was the one doing the talking. . . . So I said, 'I'll tell you what, Coach, you keep saying no to me and you won't let me talk.' I said, 'Let me tell you something, you're wearing that World Championship ring, and if I had not made that interception, we would not be wearing that championship ring.' . . . He said, 'Bullshit!' . . . I said, 'What do you mean, bullshit?' . . . He said, 'The fact of the matter is anybody could have made that interception.' . . . I said, 'Coach, I don't think so. . . . I made it. . . . I want my five thousand dollars.' . . . He said, 'No! . . . Get out of my office.' . . . So I said, 'That's it?' And he said, 'That's it.' So I get up and I go to the door and I grab the knob to open the door, and he says, 'By the way, kid, if you're thinking of leaving camp, the fine is normally one hundred dollars a day, but for you . . . I'll make it two hundred dollars a day. . . . Have a nice night!' I remember that like it was yesterday. That was in 1964 going into training camp in Rensselaer."

LEO GEORGE (Bill George's son): "Fred Williams told me a great story about negotiating with Halas. He said Halas would keep records of the players' performances each game and grade them. Fred went in to see him one year, intent on getting a raise. George Halas brought this book out and showed it to him and said, 'You don't deserve a raise. You're not worthy of it because this is the kind of year you had. Absolutely not.' Well, the next year Fred Williams led the team in tackles and was voted to the Pro Bowl. He went back into Halas's office, ready to go at it for a raise. Williams said to Halas, 'You know, Coach, you said last year I couldn't have a raise, but you kept that book, the one on top of your cabinet there. Let's get that book down now and see how it looks this year. I want a raise.' Halas stares at him and says, 'That book doesn't mean a damn thing, Fred. It means nothing at all.' Fred says, 'If you're not going to give me a raise, then trade me.' Halas says, 'I've been trying for years, kid. Nobody wants your sorry ass.' Fred told that story many times."

STAN JONES (Defensive Tackle): "Well, I played thirteen years, and it took me thirteen years to earn $130,000. If it hadn't been for my last year with the Redskins, I wouldn't have made that. I went down there, and they asked me if they could work a trade out, how much I wanted. I thought, 'Well, I might as well shoot for the moon.' I said, 'Twenty thousand dollars,' and they said yes."

LEO GEORGE (Bill George's son): "You look at the contracts the players are signing today out of college. I remember my father told me that he and Fred Williams, when they signed their first contract with the Bears, they bought a shotgun. That was their bonus—they bought a shotgun."

MIKE DITKA (Tight End): "I came to Chicago from the East-West All-Star game where I changed planes. George Allen got on the plane and went back to Pittsburgh with me. I had been drafted by Houston in the AFL, and I met with them and talked with them and they had offered me about four times the money the Bears did. We were in our livingroom, my dad, my mom, me, and George Allen. He got Halas on the phone, and you know, of course, George was George. 'Well this is the highest contract I've ever offered anybody. Oh, this is the most bonus money we have paid anybody since Red Grange.' I knew he was lying about that, but what are you going to do? I remember I asked my dad what he thought. He said, 'Son, I think it's more than fair.' Of course, considering what he made working in the mill, it was a lot of money. He said, 'Well, why don't you just take it?' I said okay, and I did the deal. Following my rookie year, after I had made Rookie of the Year and caught more passes than any other tight end had ever caught, I was looking to get a raise when I went into see him. He said, 'You had a good year, kid' then he pulled out that book he kept. 'You broke curfew . . . you were late to a couple of meetings . . . I saw you in that bar.' He had all that stuff written down. Finally he said, 'I'm going to give you fourteen thousand dollars.' I said, 'Whoa, wait a second, I made eighteen last year.' He said, 'No, you made twelve.' I said, 'I made eighteen . . . twelve salary and six bonus is eighteen. I'll be damned if I'll sign for a penny less than eighteen.' He filled out a contract for eighteen, and just like a dummy I signed it. That was a lot of money. What I'm saying is that that was an experience these players today will never understand. They have lawyers and agents who go in for them and negotiate everything. When you as a player have to negotiate one on one with one of the founders of the National Football League, you have got to pat yourself on the back if you come out alive."

Gene "Big Daddy" Lipscomb. Baltimore Colts game program.

15

Here Come the Colts Again!

The Baltimore Colts, entering their game against Chicago on Sunday, trailed the Bears and Green Bay by three games. Just four weeks ago the Colts had lost a hard-fought game to the Bears at Wrigley Field, 10–3. In that game, Baltimore played without its two best receivers, Raymond Berry and Jimmy Orr. In 1962, Berry had caught fifty-five passes for three touchdowns, while the fleet-footed Orr had scored a team-high eleven touchdowns on fifty-five catches. Both would be welcome additions to the offensive unit.

The Colts in 1963 were trying to recapture the magic of the late 1950s. The classic championship games with the New York Giants, in 1958 and 1959, had brought them and professional football to the forefront of American sports. On paper all the star players were still in place. Unitas, Berry, Lenny Moore, Gino Marchetti, and Jim Parker were all still productive players, but the quality and depth at the other positions were lacking. Gone from the glory years were team leaders Allen Ameche, Jim Mutscheller on offense, and bookend tackles Art Donovan and Gene "Big Daddy" Lipscomb on defense. Donovan, at 6'3", 270 pounds, had been a strong, agile player for his size. Clogging the middle of the Colts' defensive line, he made it difficult for opponents to run inside. Working together, Gino Marchetti and Donovan formed one of the best pass-rush combinations in football history.

Always amiable and witty off the field, Donovan's one-liners kept his teammates loose in the locker room. The son of famous boxing referee Art Donovan Sr., this former Boston College star was highly respected throughout his career for his dedication to the game of football.

WEEB EWBANK (Coach, Baltimore Colts): "Art was a pro's pro. He was always trying to improve. He had that one thing every great athlete must have: pride."

STAN JONES (Defensive Tackle): "When I played on offense early in my career, Art Donovan was always the toughest tackle for me to block. He was not only big, he was quick. He was like a matador. He'd move one way, then the other. Art was the smartest tackle I ever faced. He was my role model when I moved to defense."

On the other side of the Colts' defense was Gene Lipscomb, who was the first renowned physical specimen in the NFL. Standing 6'6", 305 pounds, Big Daddy was blessed with excellent size, speed, and strength. Not regarded as a strong pass rusher, Lipscomb maintained his position at the line of scrimmage until he diagnosed the play, then he would run it down with his quickness.

This mountain of a man never played football in college, but caught the attention of the Los Angeles Rams while playing football in the marines in 1953. Signed to a contract by then Rams PR director Pete Rozelle, Lipscomb played three years with Los Angeles before being let go in 1955 for his inconsistent play and problems off the field. The Colts, in need of a defensive lineman, signed him to a contract in 1956.

The Colts' head coach, Weeb Ewbank, right from the start made Lipscomb his project. Ewbank would go out of his way to build Lipscomb up to the media, and as a result Big Daddy's work ethic and performance improved. In the five years Lipscomb spent with the Colts, he was voted to two Pro Bowls and two All-League teams.

In 1961, the Colts traded him to the Pittsburgh Steelers. A heavy drinker, Big Daddy had a voracious appetite for food, women, and having a good time. "He'd pour himself a water glass full of whiskey and drink it down like other people drink soda pop," said former teammate Johnny Sample. Lipscomb for fun liked to drive around in his yellow Cadillac convertible, looking for a good time. On May 10, 1963, Big

Daddy found more than he bargained for and died of a heroin overdose. Not known as a drug user, friends and colleagues were puzzled by the cause of his death.

ART ROONEY (Owner, Pittsburgh Steelers, 1963): "I believe somebody did that to him. The Steelers never had any sign of heroin use. He drank—no question about that. But there was never a sign of anything else. What I believe happened is he was drinking, probably fooling around with some girls or whomever. They shot him up, figuring he'd be a great guy to get hooked, and he died of an overdose."

Although it was never proved that Lipscomb was murdered, his autopsy did reveal that his liver was in bad shape from a lifetime of heavy drinking. It was just a matter of time before he would have been incapacitated by a bad liver. He was thirty-two years old when he died.

GENE "BIG DADDY" LIPSCOMB (Defensive Tackle): "I wonder if those cats up there on the moon have a football team. If they do, Big Daddy would have himself a ball. When those scientists look at the planet at night and see somebody making tackles all over the surface, they'll be able to say, 'There's the man in the moon, and it's Big Daddy Lipscomb."

Bears halfback Ronnie Bull, following the Eagles game, had spent the night in a Chicago hospital. Kicked in the head in the second quarter, he watched the remainder of the game on the sidelines. Suffering severe headaches, he was taken to the hospital for precautionary reasons. With the headaches gone, Bull was released the next day and was looking forward to getting back in the lineup. The second-year player was fast establishing himself as one of the best young backs in the NFL. He had proven to be a very capable runner, with speed to turn the corner, and was a very reliable pass receiver. His 44-yard run off a short Rudy Bukich pass had been the difference in the first Colts game. Bull, with a now healthy Willie Galimore, gave the Bears a great tandem at halfback.

RONNIE BULL (Halfback): "I don't think I could have ever played football just for money. The game had to be fun for me, or I wouldn't have played."

The Colts would be out to avenge last year's home loss to the Bears, 57–0. George Halas, expecting this game to be much tougher, began his spin on the game to the media on Monday. "Golly, we know we will really be in for it. Undoubtedly this will be our toughest game of the year. We had a heck of a time beating them at home," he exclaimed to the press. "The Colts are much healthier this week than they were the last time. I'm very concerned about this game. We will have to play our best football of the year, just to have a chance of winning." Chicago would go into the game a three-point favorite.

The game plan against the Colts was pretty simple: keep Johnny Unitas and the explosive Colt offense off the field. Unitas had completed 21 of 36 passes for 210 yards in the first game against Chicago, but the Colts had scored no touchdowns. With the addition of Berry and Orr, it was foolhardy to think that Baltimore wouldn't find the end zone in this game. The Bears' offense would need to put some sustained drives together, forcing the Colts' offense to watch much of the game from the sidelines.

Chicago, in typical fashion, lost the coin toss for the eighth consecutive time to start the ball game. Baltimore, looking sharp, moved quickly into Bears territory. Unitas, relying on the running of Lenny Moore and the sure hands of Raymond Berry, reached the Bears' 28-yard line before Chicago's defense finally stiffened. Jim Martin's field-goal attempt missed badly to the left.

The Chicago offense, on the field for the first time, ran two dive plays that netted just three yards, setting up a third and seven. Wade dropped back to pass but was almost sacked by blitzing linebacker Andy Nelson. Rolling out of Nelson's grasp, Wade sidestepped crashing end Ordelle Brasse and tossed the ball to a wide-open Joe Marconi. Marconi caught the ball 5 yards past the line of scrimmage and took off down the field. Picking up a couple of blocks, he broke into the clear at his own 40-yard line. Following a convoy of blockers, the big fullback lumbered toward the end zone. Beginning to tire, he was hit by a diving Jim Welsh at the Colts' 22-yard line and knocked out-of-bounds. The pass play had gained 63 yards.

The Bears, quickly huddling, went back to the ground game, where three straight running plays advanced the ball to the Colts' 1-yard line. Wade, on a quarterback sneak, dove over for the touchdown. Bob Jencks's extra point made it 7–0.

Both defenses dominated play the rest of the first half, as neither team could produce any points. Unitas, under constant pressure, was sacked twice, stopping Baltimore drives. The Bears', playing conservatively with a seven-point lead, picked up a few first downs, but could not get past midfield. Chicago headed to the locker room at halftime in front, 7–0.

Early in the third period, Unitas attempted to pass and was intercepted by Joe Fortunato. The Bears' defensive captain returned the ball to the Colts' 25-yard line. It was the defense's twenty-third interception of the season.

The Chicago offense went right to work. First, little-used back Charlie Bivins gained 5 yards off-tackle. Then Wade hit Rick Casares on a short pass in the flat. Casares broke free from linebacker Nelson, then ran over Colt defender Lenny Lyles at the 5-yard line, en route to the Bears' second touchdown. Jencks's kick expanded the lead to 14–0.

The Colts' offense was now desperate to make something happen and struck quickly. Beginning from their own 30-yard line, the Colts scored in just seven plays, culminating with a 25-yard dash by halfback Lenny Moore. Martin's kick cut the Bears' lead to 14–7.

Baltimore valiantly tried to come back, but each time the Bears' defense responded. Early in the fourth quarter, with Baltimore driving into Chicago territory, Larry Morris recovered a Unitas fumble. Later in the last period, Baltimore faced fourth and one at the Bears' 24-yard line. A Unitas quarterback sneak came up one inch short of the first down. Near the end of the game, the Bears scored once more, on Roger LeClerc's 12-yard field goal. The final score was 17–7.

The Bears, now 7–1, had again controlled the Colts' offense, allowing just one touchdown. Baltimore, in losing to the Bears for the sixth consecutive time, had turned the ball over three times. Unitas had completed 11 of 19 passing attempts, but for only 90 yards and no touchdowns. His frustration was evident in the Colts' locker room following the game.

JOHNNY UNITAS (Quarterback, Baltimore Colts): "These losses are so hard, when we don't take advantage of our scoring opportunities. Each week we figure out ways to lose games, rather than win

Old foes . . . old friends. *Left to right:* John Unitas, Dan Sullivan, Maury Youmans, and Paul Charlebois. Courtesy of Maury Youmans.

them. One of these weeks that's going to change. The Bears are a good team, but we sure seem to make it easy for them."

The Bears' defense sacked Unitas four times, for minus 37 yards. In giving up seven points, the combined total of points allowed through eight games stood at eighty-two. No other team was remotely close to that number.

Bill Wade, again solid at quarterback, had completed 9 passes on only 12 attempts. The Bears rushed for 164 yards, picking up 18 first downs. George Halas was pleased with his starting quarterback and the offense in general. "We did a great job on offense today. I thought our guys showed what they are made of. That Bill Wade is playing quarterback as well as anybody in the league. I'm glad to get this one behind us. Those Colts are a good team, I don't care what anybody says and they will win their share of games the rest of the year. It will be good to go play at home for a change."

The Bears would have five out of their last six games at home. Next week would be the rematch with the L.A. Rams, before the biggest game of the year, against the Green Bay Packers. Halas would make sure his players didn't look ahead, even though the Packers were already on his radar screen. This could finally be the year his team returned to glory. This could be revenge against his hated rival. . . . This could be . . . This could . . . The old man smiled.

Roger LeCLERC

KICKER

Doug Atkins brought a notebook to training camp in 1963. He would sit in the meeting taking notes. All of us players thought it was funny . . . of all people taking notes, Doug Atkins, because he was usually sleeping through the meetings. But he would sit there, jotting things down. I said, 'Doug, what are you doing?' He said, 'I'm taking notes of what the coaches are saying.' After a few weeks he stopped writing. I asked him, 'Doug, why did you quit writing?' He said, 'I got sick of writing the same thing down day after day.'

"Joe Fortunato at the weigh-ins would get behind a player and lift them up by the cheeks of their rear end to make them lighter. Earl Leggett and him became good friends at the weigh-in."

Roger LeClerc. Courtesy of Chicago Bears.

Roger LeClerc providing the offense against the Los Angeles Rams.
Courtesy of Roger LeClerc.

16

Rams Invade!

The win over the Colts improved the Bears' record to 7–1, and with five of their six remaining games at home, Chicago had a favorable schedule to finish the season. Most experts were now picking the Bears to win the Western Conference. One expert who didn't subscribe to that theory was George Halas. "Over-all I don't think there's much difference playing at home or on the road. Oh, don't get me wrong, I think the home crowd can help, but when you're on the road you have certain advantages too. First you have better control of the team, all staying at the same place. You don't get involved with a lot of petty things that can distract you, like phone calls for tickets, and things like that. You also have an opportunity to have more meetings on the road." Papa Bear wanted no talk that would suggest his team had an advantage over Green Bay going down the stretch. Any detail that could cause complacency among his players was forbidden. Each game would be a war, taken one game at a time. He would have it no other way.

The Green Bay Packers kept pace with the Bears by defeating the Pittsburgh Steelers on the road, 33–14. The Packers, prior to next week's rematch with the Bears, would host Minnesota on Sunday. The defending champions would have only the 49ers left at home, with road games to Chicago, Detroit, Los Angeles, and San Francisco, a very tough schedule to finish the season.

Zeke Bratkowski. Courtesy of Chicago Bears.

Concerned about the quarterback position, Vince Lombardi had added quarterback Zeke Bratkowski to his team's roster. He was pleased to acquire the veteran quarterback for the economic waiver fee of one hundred dollars.

A big part of the Bears' success thus far this season had been in the turnover department. On defense they created them, but the offense rarely turned the ball over. There had been few fumbles lost through the first eight games, with only seven Chicago passes being intercepted. Bill Wade was ranked third among quarterbacks, completing more than 60 percent of his passes. No other Bear player cracked the top five in any statistical category.

Roosevelt Taylor had been outstanding on the Bears' defensive unit, leading the team in tackles and interceptions (with four). Besides playing defense, Taylor returned punts and was a member of the kickoff team. Lining up next to kicker Bob Jencks, it was Taylor's job to lag behind, prepared to run down any returner who happened to break loose from the pack. At 5'11", weighing only 186 pounds, he made up for his lack of size with his strong determination to be a professional football player.

ROOSEVELT TAYLOR (Defensive Back): "When I left Grambling College, I was able to get a tryout with the Bears as a free agent. The Bears were mostly interested in me because of my college teammate Ernie Ladd. They thought that if they signed me to a free-agent contract, then perhaps they could also get Ernie Ladd under contract. Ernie went to the AFL, but I went up there and won a job. I started out by impressing the coaches by winning the 'Halas Mile.' George Allen was always in my corner, telling Halas to give me a chance. He finally did and I won a spot on the team. Up until that first training camp I had never seen a professional game."

The Rams, after being soundly defeated a few weeks before by the Bears, had won two of their last three games. L.A. coach Harland Svare had decided to give young quarterback Roman Gabriel his chance to start and released starter Zeke Bratkowski. Gabriel at 6'4", 224 pounds, had the size and arm to be an outstanding quarterback in the NFL. Through three games it appeared that Svare had made the right decision, as the team was averaging more than twenty points per game with Gabriel at quarterback.

The Rams on defense were beginning to jell as a defensive unit. Led by veteran tackle Roosevelt Grier, this young, talented group included Deacon Jones, Merlin Olsen, and Lamar Lundy. The Bears' defensive coordinator, George Allen, thought they were the most talented line the Bears would play against all year. "That front wall has the ability to get after people. I am amazed at their size and quickness. Early in the season they were under achieving, but they appear to be coming into their own." George Halas echoed his young defensive coordinator's sentiments: "They are four of the largest defensive linemen I've ever seen on one team, and I'm sure we'll have to be at our best to cope with them." Averaging 276 pounds in weight and more than 6'6" in height, they were a challenge for any offensive unit.

Ronnie Bull continued to have injury problems, as he suffered a sprained ankle in the Bears' win over the Colts. His availability for the Rams game was again in doubt. The Bears did get some good news when two of their injured defensive players were activated. First, Ed O'Bradovich was finally cleared to play after spending the first eight weeks of the season on injured reserve. The second-year player out of Illinois had suffered from a variety of ailments that had kept him on the sidelines. Credited with sixty-two tackles and five fumble recoveries his rookie year, his presence in the lineup would be a great addition to the defense. Also the Bears activated defensive tackle Fred Williams, who had been out with a shoulder separation. The veteran tackle had been a solid player for the Bears over the years, and his presence would again give the Bears great depth along the front line.

For the first time all season, the Bears won the toss and elected to receive to begin the game. The offense steadily moved down the field, primarily off the strong running of Willie Galimore and Joe Marconi. Pushing deep into Rams territory, two holding penalties stalled the drive. Roger LeClerc came on to boot a 30-yard field goal to give the Bears a 3–0 lead.

The Los Angeles offense, minus its two best running backs, Jon Arnett and Dick Bass, could not get untracked to begin the game. Constant pressure by the Bears' defense, led by rookie tackle John Johnson, kept the Rams' offense off balance. Roman Gabriel was sacked repeatedly and was hurried on almost every throw. The Rams were forced to punt three times in the first quarter.

The Bears' offense, which had looked so good in its first possession, began to have problems moving the ball. The Rams' big front line began to take control of the line of scrimmage. Running backs Galimore and Marconi could no longer find running room and were constantly being hit behind the line of scrimmage. Halas, frustrated in the second quarter by his team's inability to move the ball, replaced Wade with Bukich, but his presence in the lineup didn't help. The Rams went to the locker room behind by only three points.

The third quarter began similarly to the way the first half had ended, with each team exchanging punts. In the Bears' second possession, Wade (back in the game) connected with Mike Ditka on a beautiful 15-yard sideline pass to give the Bears an important first down. Wade, calling an audible at the line of scrimmage, completed a swing pass to Galimore, who romped 44 yards downfield before being tackled by the Rams' Carver Shannon at the Rams' 24-yard line. Wade again changed the play at the line of scrimmage and went back to the air, hitting a diving Johnny Morris for 9 yards. Svare, feeling the game slipping away, decided to call time-out to give his big line a chance to rest and regroup. The decision paid off as the Bears could advance the ball only 5 more yards before being forced to kick another field goal. LeClerc's 16-yard field goal extended the Bears' lead to 6–0.

Chicago's defense continued to play well, not allowing the Rams to cross midfield. With less than four minutes to play in the fourth quarter, the Bears began a drive from their own 30-yard line. Wade opened the drive with a 9-yard completion to John Farrington. Then Charlie Bivins, on two sensational runs, advanced the ball 30 yards to give Chicago a first down inside the Rams' 30-yard line. With the clock now ticking down inside two minutes, the Bears reached the 13-yard line. Three running plays netted 7 yards, placing the ball at the Rams' 6-yard line. On fourth down, Roger LeClerc came in to ice the game for Chicago.

Los Angeles's outstanding linebacker Jack Pardee lined up to the right of center for the field-goal try by the Bears. As the ball was snapped, Pardee rushed up the middle untouched, extending his arms, and hit the ball flush, knocking it backward, and it bounced crazily in the opposite direction. Players from both sides converged toward the loose pigskin, diving to recover it, but each time pushing it closer toward the Bears' goal line. By the time the ball was downed, it was marked inside the Bears' 40-yard line. The Rams, who looked to be totally out of the game, were presented one golden opportunity to steal a victory, with forty-two seconds left on the game clock.

The Bears' defensive unit, brilliant all day, would be called upon once more to save the game. The players trotting back on the field were in shock at the turn of events. Doug Atkins, angry at the kicking team for allowing such a bizarre situation like this to happen, berated every member of the group he could find. On first down Atkins, still fuming, head-slapped Rams lineman Joe Scibelli, knocking him to the ground, and converged on Roman Gabriel. Halfback Ben Wilson now in his way, Atkins hit Wilson with a forearm that knocked Wilson backward into Gabriel, forcing him to stumble out of the pocket. Gabriel, now chased by Atkins, wildly threw downfield, overthrowing a wide-open Jim Phillips at the goal line. There were twenty-nine seconds remaining to play. On second down Gabriel took a three-step drop and hit Phillips quickly on a sideline pattern for 8 yards. On third down Gabriel hit tight end Marlin McKeever for 9 yards and a first down. The Rams used their last time-out to stop the clock, with thirteen seconds remaining. Breaking the huddle, Gabriel knew he had to get the ball to the end zone. He hoped his offensive line could give him time to do that. Gabriel took the snap and rolled out away from Doug Atkins. Looking downfield, he threw toward Phillips at the 5-yard line. Richie Petibone, closing fast from his corner position, knocked the ball away as Phillips reached out to grab it. The Rams had time for one more play. The Bears' defense huddled for the last time in the game. They knew they could not afford a loss to the Rams. It would be devastating.

Roman Gabriel received the play from the sideline and quickly brought his team to the line of scrimmage. Bears middle linebacker Bill George, quickly recognizing the Rams' formation, motioned outside linebacker Larry Morris to move three steps toward the middle. On the snap, George broke to the inside rather than move backward in pass coverage. The Rams, not expecting a blitz, failed to block George as he sprinted toward Gabriel. The rookie quarterback saw George coming, but it was too late to avoid him. George hit Gabriel around the shoulder, spinning him around. The big quarterback, with George on him, frantically spun around, shaking loose. Gabriel instinctively turned and blindly lofted a pass toward the back right of the end zone, where he hoped one of his receivers would be. Roosevelt Taylor from the middle of the field broke toward the corner as the ball was released by the Rams' quarterback. Leaping in front of Jim Phillips, Taylor with one arm extended batted the ball away, preserving the Bears' victory. Chicago had held on to win 6–0.

A very tired Bill Wade following the game just shook his head on the closeness of the contest. "Give the Rams credit, they sure played us tough this time. I thought at the beginning of the game we were going to have a big day on offense, but unfortunately that didn't happen. Give the defense the cheers for bailing us out today. They held the Rams to less than 100 yards which is phenomenal." When asked why the Chicago offense had failed to score a touchdown in their first drive, he offered this insight: "The Rams were stunting and I called an audible but didn't have enough time to get the play off. That and the penalty definitely hurt us. Other than that last drive, we never really got untracked after that."

Rookie John Johnson, playing in place of the injured Stan Jones, had played outstandingly and was awarded the game ball. George Halas, unusually subdued following the win, had this to say about the closeness of the game: "This was a different Rams team, than the one we walloped a few weeks ago. Their defense played a tremendous game. Yes this Rams team has come a long way since we first played them."

The Bears now looked forward to the biggest game of the year next week, the rematch with the Green Bay Packers.

BILL WADE (Quarterback): "The last game I had with the Los Angeles Rams was when we played the Colts. I ran 66 yards for a touchdown—the only touchdown of the game. Years later I get a call from a reporter, and he told me that I had held an NFL record for thirty-five years for the longest run from scrimmage by a quarterback. Kordell Stewart later ran for 80 yards. I never even knew it was kept as a record. I wanted to win the game, and that was the only touchdown of the game."

J. C. Caroline. Courtesy of Chicago Bears.

17

Wrigley Will Be Rocking

THE PACK IS BACK!

*George Halas never called me before games, but the
night before our game against Green Bay, he calls me
around 11:00 p.m. Halas says, "Joe, what does it look
like for the game?" I said, "Well, Coach, we got all
the defensive signals ready. I feel pretty good about
everything." He said, "I'm glad to hear that." Then
I told him, "Coach, I'm going to tell you something
right now. If they keep doing what they have been
doing off the scouting reports we have on them, we
may shut them out." He didn't say a thing for a
minute or so. Finally, he said, "Joe, are you kidding
me?" I said, "No, I'm serious about that, Coach."
There was another long pause, then Halas said,
"Good night, kid. Get some rest." He then hung up
the phone.*

—Joe Fortunato, linebacker

The game of the year was in place for Chicago and Green Bay, following both teams' victories the previous Sunday. The Bears' fortunate win over the Rams, 6–0, coupled with the Packers' pasting of
Minnesota, 28–7, set up the contest for first place in the Western Con-

ference. The winner would have a decided advantage as to who would advance to the NFL Championship game.

Green Bay over the past few years had dominated the series between the two teams. In 1962 the Packers beat the Bears twice, 49–0 at Green Bay followed by a 38–7 thrashing in Chicago. Bears fans would have to go back to 1958 to find a season that the Bears were able to defeat the Packers twice in one year. Since Vince Lombardi became the head coach in Green Bay in 1959, the Packers had won six of the last nine games played. The challenge to defeat this powerful team twice in one year would be a monumental task for the Bears.

The Packers were installed as a four-point favorite early in the week, and Bears coach George Halas couldn't have agreed more. "On past performance, the fact that they are the world champions and have handled us so easy the past few years, you would have to make them the favorite to win. Psychologically, I think that 10–3 licking we gave them also will give them an edge." The Bears' coach also defended his offensive team, which was under heavy criticism for not being able to score any touchdowns against the Rams. "We'd like to score more points, so would the other teams too," Halas said. "The defenses are getting bigger and sharper. It's unrealistic to expect our team to pile up points, while our team keeps stopping the opponent." Bears offensive backfield coach Chuck Mather also came to the aid of the offense:

"I'm not the least disappointed in our offense, certainly not their play against the Rams. Much of the time it depends on how the defense plays and the Rams defense played great. No team in the league has a better four-man rush than they do at this time. Also when evaluating our offense, you need to take into consideration that we make very few mistakes. We have had very few fumbles, and very little pass interceptions. Our quarterbacks are rarely sacked, because we have the best pass protection in the league. So when you're evaluating an offense you need to include all those things in your evaluation."

In Green Bay much of the talk was about the health of Bart Starr, as the injured quarterback had begun practicing again with the team. Starr's leadership and his experience in big games were factors that could help determine the game's outcome. "Starr has a real good chance of playing," Lombardi told the media. "The splints are off.

He's been handling the ball from under center, and his passes look real good. A lot to him being able to play will be up to the weather this week and how much of a chance he will get to work outside."

John Roach, thrust into the starting lineup with Starr's injury, had played well. Last week in the win over the Minnesota Vikings he had completed 12 of 20 passes, for 112 yards and 3 touchdowns. Lombardi was impressed with Roach's performance but hoped that Starr would be able to play in such an important game.

The Bears players were low-key in their approach to the upcoming game. Each player was confident that the team would be ready for the challenge of beating the Packers twice. The pressure of playing in such an important game did not seem to affect them.

JOE FORTUNATO (Linebacker): "Each player gets ready for a game differently. We seldom get pep talks from Halas. Pro players don't need pep talks to get ready to play."

The Bears' star receiver Johnny Morris also spoke out about the offense while presenting his thoughts on the upcoming game. "Look maybe we're not scoring a lot of points on offense but we are controlling the ball. I think it will take twenty points to win this game. If we can get ahead, we will win. If they get ahead, I don't know."

Most experts thought the game would be low scoring, because of both teams' outstanding defenses. Each team was ranked near the top in all defensive categories, so points on Sunday should again be at a premium.

George Allen and his staff spent the first part of the week reviewing over and over the vast amount of information they had on the Green Bay offense. Allen's meticulous approach to football included keeping updated notebooks on each opponent that broke down each of their offensive plays. Allen then would transfer this information onto three-by-five-inch cards, which he would use in his development of the Bears' defensive game plan. Allen knew this Green Bay offense better than any person outside the Green Bay organization. Watching endless hours of Green Bay games over the past months, the young coach was confident his defense would be prepared for whatever the Packers tried to throw at them. He was looking forward to matching wits with the great Vince Lombardi.

In the offensive room, assistant coach Jim Dooley had also been watching hours of Green Bay film. Dooley determined that he could decipher when the Packers were blitzing by the movement of two of their players, Willie Wood and Ray Nitschke. Dooley determined that linebacker Ray Nitschke would start moving his feet prior to the snap if he was going to blitz. Second, Willie Wood, the Packers' great defensive back, would turn a certain way depending on if he was blitzing or covering a receiver. Given this information, quarterback Bill Wade could make adjustments at the line of scrimmage. This would give the offense a distinct advantage against this great defensive team. George Halas hoped this edge would translate into his team scoring some points.

Green Bay typically arrived in Chicago the day before the game, holding a short afternoon practice at Wrigley Field. This year Lombardi decided to change his team's schedule. His team would practice Saturday morning in Green Bay, then bus down to Chicago. The Green Bay coach all week in preparation for the Bears had kept his team's practices closed. When asked about the unusually tight security, Lombardi laughed it off, saying, "Listen, we're not putting anything fancy in for this game. If the Bears beat us, they will beat us at what we do best. We're not going to make any big changes for this game." The Green Bay coach, attempting to play down the magnitude of the game, added, "After Sunday's game there are still four games to go. We and the Bears each have a game against Detroit, a team that will have a lot to say about the race. By no means will this thing be decided in Chicago, although a victory would certainly ease things."

Green Bay's tough middle linebacker Ray Nitschke summed up his thoughts about the game: "There is no team I would rather beat than the Bears. Our team will be ready this time, because this is for all the marbles. We don't like Chicago."

On November 17, 1963, a record crowd of 49,166 jammed Wrigley Field to watch the Bears and Packers do battle for first place in the Western Conference. The Bears, sending team captains Stan Jones and Bill George out to midfield, lost the coin flip for the ninth time in ten tries. The Packers elected to receive.

Bob Jencks's end-over-end kick reached the goal line, where Herb

Adderly gathered it in. Quickly breaking to his right, Adderly reached the 10-yard line, where he spotted a wall of blockers forming up the sideline. Switching the ball to his right arm, Adderly accelerated his speed, prepared to sprint up the sideline, possibly for a long run. Suddenly, out of the corner of his eye he saw a Chicago player converging on him. The Green Bay speedster, now reaching the 15-yard line, looked for someone to block this incoming missile, but it was too late. J. C. Caroline hit Adderly at full speed, knocking him down at the 17-yard line. Adderly was dazed from the fierce contact, but somehow managed to hang on to the ball. Green Bay would be forced to begin the game inside their own 20-yard line. They would begin this important game with John Roach at quarterback. Bart Starr's ailing wrist still was not strong enough to allow him to play. He would watch this game from the Green Bay sidelines.

John Roach received last-minute instructions from Vince Lombardi, then trotted on the field to direct the Green Bay offense. The Bears, lining up in their 4–3 defense, attacked the line of scrimmage with a vengeance. Chicago's front wall stopped fullback Jim Taylor on two consecutive off-tackle runs. Roach on third down, flushed out of the pocket, completed a 12-yard strike to Max McGee to give the Packers a first down at the Chicago 29-yard line. The Packers on first down ran wide, but Larry Morris knocked Taylor down after a short 2-yard gain. Green Bay, still playing conservatively, ran Tom Moore off-tackle for another 2 yards, setting up another third-down play. This time Roach overthrew a wide-open Boyd Dowler at the Bears' 45-yard line. Green Bay punter Jerry Norton, under tremendous pressure, hit a poor punt that rolled out-of-bounds at the Bears' 40-yard line.

On first down Bears fullback Joe Marconi burst up the middle for 9 yards. Then halfback Willie Galimore gained 6 yards around the left end to give the Bears a first down inside Green Bay territory. Deciding to go to the air, Bill Wade faked a dive to Marconi, then found Mike Ditka wide open across the middle for 16 yards and another Chicago first down. Green Bay, reeling from the two first downs, held the Bears on three successive plays, forcing the Bears to attempt a field goal. Roger LeClerc's 29-yard try was perfect to give the Bears an early 3–0 lead.

The Packers, unable to move the ball against the fired-up Bears defense, were again forced to punt. Norton's second poor effort went out-of-bounds at the Chicago 39-yard line.

The Bears, back on offense, continued to grind it out through the strong running of Marconi and Galimore. Steadily moving the Green Bay defense backward, the Bears pushed again into field-goal range. Similar to the first drive, LeClerc came on to kick another field goal, this time from 46 yards, to extend the Bears' lead to 6–0.

Chicago's third kickoff of the day was fielded by Herb Adderly at the Packer 5-yard line. This time Adderly headed straight up the middle, but found some open room to his right created by a huge block by Bob Skoronski. Now at full speed, he motored up the sideline 15 yards before he was forced to cut back toward the middle. The Bears' John Farrington, on the opposite side of the field, was also moving toward the middle of the field. Farrington, avoiding one block, hit Adderly from the blind side, stripping the ball from the returner. The ball bounced free and was pounced on by Roger LeClerc at the Green Bay 36-yard line. Chicago, leading by six points, had the first big break in the game.

The Bears moved quickly against the stunned Packers, reaching the Green Bay 27-yard line on two running plays. The Packer defense, bending but not breaking all day, was being called on here to make a big stand. Wade at the line of scrimmage changed the play, now deciding to run a sweep with Willie Galimore. The veteran back, taking the pitch wide, saw little running room to the outside. Quickly he sliced back toward the middle, where he slid past a diving Henry Jordan, then sidestepped his way back outside, away from the grasp of Ray Nitschke. With Packer defender Jesse Whittenton in his path, "Willie the Wisp" turned on the juice, and flew by the Packer defender like he was standing still. Galimore crossed the Packer goal as Wrigley Field erupted in cheers. Bob Jencks's extra point gave the Bears a 13–0 lead.

Vince Lombardi on the Packers' sideline was incredulous. His Packers, always dominant when it counted, were giving the game away.

Green Bay settled down after the touchdown but continued to have problems moving the ball against the Bears' defense. Neither team scored as the first half came to a close.

To begin the third quarter the Bears took the kickoff and marched down the field, again using the short pass and the running game as their most effective weapons. The Packer defense, again bending, gave up their third field goal of the game, to give the Bears a 16–0 lead. Neither team could move the ball the remainder of the quarter.

Now totally frustrated with the inept play of his offense, Lombardi inserted newly acquired Zeke Bratkowski into the game at quarterback. Bratkowski, under a heavy Bears rush, was hit just as he aimed a pass at Max McGee. The ball fluttered in the air and was picked off at the Packer 35-yard line by Bears defender Dave Whitsell, giving the Bears another great scoring opportunity. Unable to generate any more offense against the Packers, Chicago settled for Roger LeClerc's 42-yard field goal to give the Bears a commanding 19–0 lead.

The Bears five minutes later put the game away. Bratkowski, again under pressure, tried to force a pass to tight end Ron Kramer at midfield, but was picked off by Bennie McRae. Catching the ball in stride, McRae wove his way down to the Packer 5-yard line where he was wrestled to the ground by Forrest Gregg. On the second play from scrimmage, Wade ran to his right and dove into the end zone for the touchdown. Jencks's kick made the score 26–0.

The game now decided, the Packers did score a touchdown on their next possession, highlighted by a 64-yard completion from Bratkowski to Max McGee. When the gun sounded, ending the game, the Bears were the victors 26–7.

The Bears had systematically destroyed the Packers with their ball-control offense and a smothering defense. "We played their type of game and beat them at it today," said Bill Wade in the jubilant Bears locker room following the game. "The New York Giants are the fathers of this type of ball-control game. The Packers took it up, and now we try to play the same type of game. It may not be as spectacular but you get results," Wade added. The Bears for the second time had shut down the high-powered Green Bay offense. Averaging 33 points per game against the rest of the NFL in 1963, the Packers could score a total of only 10 points in their two losses to Chicago. Green Bay turned the ball over seven times on two fumbles and five interceptions. The Bears had no turnovers for the game.

"Control the ball with runs and short passes," remarked Halas about his team's strategy against the Green Bay defense. "We used simple counter plays against their key defenses all afternoon." The Bears had outgained the Packers on the ground 248 yards to 71 yards for the game. Wade had completed 6 passes out of 14 attempts for only 69 yards, but each completion had been important in keeping drives alive and moving the chains. The Green Bay quarterbacks combined completed only 11 passes out of 31 attempts for 151 yards, with most of that yardage being gained on the one long pass to Max McGee. The 5 interceptions thrown by Roach and Bratkowski had contributed greatly to the Packers' defeat.

Vince Lombardi sat on a bench in the Packers' dressing room following the game, impatiently answering questions from the media. "Look, they beat the hell out of us. They beat us both ways. Their offense line beat us, and their defensive line beat us. They just beat us up front," answered the Packers' head coach. "That's all I am going to say. Ask some more questions if you want, but I am not going to say anything else." Lombardi just stared down at the floor, never looking up. His team had in his mind beaten themselves today. He had great respect for the Bears team, especially the defense, but in a year when he perhaps had his best team, they were looking up at the Bears in the standings. He could only hope that the Bears would slip, losing a couple of games somehow. He knew that probably would not happen, but at this point that's all he could hope for. The road to the championship game would not go through Green Bay this season. It was now in the control of George Halas, and his Chicago Bears.

WILLIE DAVIS (Defensive End, Green Bay Packers): "I thought we had one of our best teams in 1963. Lombardi got us so worked up before the game that I think we left everything on the practice field. We were wound up tight as a drum."

RONNIE BULL (Halfback): "One of the biggest things Jim Dooley did in 1963 was breaking down Green Bay's defense. He figured out all their keys on defense. We knew going into that game the types of defenses they would run, and when they would run them."

HENRY JORDAN (Defensive Tackle, Green Bay Packers): "If I were to answer for my ego, I would have to say no . . . the Bears are not a better team. But looking at the scores, I can't say anything but yes . . . the Bears are better. I was really impressed by their front line. Many times I was impressed right into the ground."

BILL FORRESTER (Linebacker, Green Bay Packers): "We gave 100 percent, but the trouble was the Bears gave 150 percent."

JOHNNY MORRIS (Flanker): "After every game we would have meetings and watch the game films. The special teams would watch the films together. In that Green Bay game J. C. Caroline went down on that first play and hit Adderly so hard, it set the tone for us players and the crowd at Wrigley Field. He had so many great plays that day that when the film was over, everybody in the room stood up and gave him a standing ovation. It was very emotional, all these players standing and cheering him. It's something I have never forgotten."

BOYD DOWLER (Flanker, Green Bay Packers): "We had a great team in 1963. We had worst teams in Green Bay that won championships."

Buddy Parker, head coach of the Pittsburgh Steelers. Courtesy Pittsburgh
Steelers Image Library.

18

A Nation Mourns

George Halas reported to work on Monday, November 18, 1963, knowing his Bears now had a legitimate chance of returning to the championship game, after a seven-year absence. Papa Bear savored the victory over Green Bay, but carefully selected his words in placing it in historical significance. "Yes, there have been other great moments, but you don't like to think about them at this time. You certainly don't want to take away from what is happening at this moment."

Halas understood the euphoria over such a great win but now faced the challenge of taking his team back on the road Sunday to play a very good Pittsburgh Steelers team. The Bears, now one game ahead of the Packers, must avoid any upsets in the last four games to advance to the championship game.

Of course, when it came to worrying about an opponent, nobody did it better than George Halas. "When the schedule came out last spring, I immediately checked to see what teams we were playing from the other conference. When I saw Pittsburgh, November 24th, I put a circle around the date and marked it a toughie," said a concerned Halas before practice on Wednesday. "The Steelers are at the top of their game right now, and there could be a letdown by our players after that great win over Green Bay. In John Henry Johnson they have one

Bobby Layne. Courtesy Pittsburgh Steelers Image Library.

of the best backs in all of football and in Buddy Dial, Ted Mack and Gary Ballman they have excellent receivers."

The Steelers, at 6–3–1, were still in the hunt for the Eastern Conference title, trailing the first-place New York Giants by two games. Pittsburgh had wins over the three teams currently ahead of them in the Eastern Conference, the Giants, Cleveland, and St. Louis. Coach Buddy Parker knew the importance of this game, as another loss would dash any hopes of a championship. "We need to beat the Bears on Sunday, if we want to remain in the race," Parker said. "This Bears team is very good, especially on defense where I think they have the best defensive backs in football."

Buddy Parker had become the Steelers' head coach in 1957, after a successful stint in Detroit where he led the Lions to three straight championship games beginning in 1952. In two of those years they won back-to-back crowns, before losing to Cleveland in 1954.

Parker was an expert at dissecting an opponent's strengths and weaknesses, and was highly respected by his peers for making the proper adjustments during a game. High-strung and impulsive, Parker abruptly left the Lions in 1957. Speaking at a preseason "Meet the

Lions" banquet, he told the audience, "I don't want to get into another losing season. . . . I've got a situation here I can't handle any more. . . . I'm getting out." Parker, with that said, quit that day. Then hired by the Steelers, he brought the Pittsburgh franchise back to respectability. No stranger to playing against the Bears, Parker, after reviewing one of their game films, had this to say about their style of play: "The line play was so dirty that there was a ring around the screen."

Steelers quarterback Ed Brown had been traded by the Bears to the Steelers following the 1961 season. The veteran quarterback had struggled in his first season with Pittsburgh, finally being benched and replaced by Bobby Layne. Brown, after a strong performance in preseason, had regained the starting position in 1963 and had performed well. He was especially looking forward to playing his old team on Sunday. "I want to beat them in the worst way," said a bitter Brown. "I don't think I was given a fair shot after our 1956 championship game. I was never the first string quarterback again and had to share the job with Zeke Bratkowski and later Bill Wade. After that 1961 season I was fed up and asked to be traded. Certainly this game means more than most. Everybody is a little bitter after being traded, even if you ask for it, and this is one way to get back. I have a lot of friends on that team that I came to the pro's with, and I would like to beat them. Any guy feels that way, he wants to beat the team he played for."

Struggling with nagging injuries all season, Rick Casares's season came to an abrupt end against the Green Bay Packers. The Bears' fullback had suffered an ankle separation during the fourth quarter of the game. Casares, the all-time leading rusher for the Bears entering the 1963 season, had a date to see Dr. Fox at the hospital. The date was November 22, 1963.

RICK CASARES (Fullback): "I went to the hospital to see Dr. Fox regarding my injury. All of a sudden there was this big commotion out in the hallway. Everyone was running around, all the nurses were crying, I couldn't figure out what was going on. Finally someone said the president had been shot. I couldn't believe it."

The assassination of President Kennedy changed everyone's life that cold November day. Every American was in shock over this tragedy and scrambled to pay proper respects to their fallen leader. The sports world in late November 1963 was no exception. Football, basketball, hockey, plus many other minor sports had a full schedule of games to be played. Many college football games were immediately cancelled. Conferences like the Big Ten, the Big Six, and the Ivy league all suspended play. Notre Dame cancelled its game with Iowa, and the Big Eight cancelled all its games with the exception of the Oklahoma-Nebraska game. Sooners coach Bud Wilkinson called Robert Kennedy to discuss whether to play or not. Wilkinson, who was the head of President Kennedy's physical fitness program, was encouraged to play the game by the president's brother.

After a hastily called meeting, the Southeastern Conference decided that it would play all its games. The National Hockey League also decided to play its full schedule, but the American Football League decided to cancel all its games. This now left the National Football League as the only league yet to make a decision. Commissioner Pete Rozelle, unsure of the right decision, listened carefully to the thoughts of the team owners regarding what the NFL's position should be. Still troubled over what the leagues should do, Rozelle called Bobby Kennedy to discuss the matter. Following his conversation with the attorney general, he released a statement explaining the NFL's reasons to play: "It has been traditional in sports to perform in times of great personal tragedy. Football was Mr. Kennedy's game. He thrived on competition."

Although the games would go on, the NFL decided that there would be no television, no radio, no halftime shows, and the players would not be introduced prior to the game. Because there was no directive coming from Washington regarding what the NFL and the rest of the sporting world should do, it was left up to the individual leagues, conferences, and teams to make their own decisions. Given our democratic way of life, there were strong opinions formed by Americans on which was the correct thing to do. Nonetheless, the NFL teed it up on Sunday, and all seven games were played.

BOB WETOSKA (Offensive Lineman): "I can remember coming off the practice field, coming in that door, and someone saying, 'We just heard on the radio that President Kennedy has been shot.' I remember the entire hullabaloo about whether to play the game or not.

It was a very somber time. We were driving to the stadium to play the game, and the bus driver had the radio on. It happened to be the exact time that they were transferring Oswald from the prison to someplace else. The guy on the radio was describing him coming out, and Jack Ruby shoots him. The guy said, 'My God, he's been shot.' The old man jumps up and says, 'God damn it, turn this f--king radio off!'"

On a cold, sad day in Pittsburgh, the Bears and Steelers lined up to do battle at Forbes Field, before 36,465 fans. Chicago won the toss and decided to receive. Bill Wade, directing the Bears' offense, stayed on the ground the first four plays as Joe Marconi and Ronnie Bull each carried twice for a total of 12 yards. Dropping back to pass on first down, Wade spotted John Farrington wide open. Farrington, in single coverage, was 5 yards behind Steeler defender Clendon Thomas. Wade lofted a pass toward the big receiver, who caught the ball over his shoulder at the Steelers' 35-yard line. Gathering the ball in, Farrington had an open field to the Steelers' goal line. Thomas in full pursuit caught Farrington at the 5-yard line where the two players tumbled forward, inches short of the goal line. On first down, Galimore carried over for the touchdown. Jencks's kick made it a quick 7–0.

In the second quarter, Pittsburgh's defense pressured Wade, forcing an interception. Dick Haley stepped in front of Bears receiver Johnny Morris and returned the ball 37 yards before being tackled at the Bears' 10-yard line. After an interference penalty moved the ball to the 5-yard line, Dick Hoak scored around the left end for Pittsburgh's first touchdown. Lou Michaels's kick tied the game at 7–7.

After both teams exchanged punts, Chicago put another scoring drive together. Starting at their own 37-yard line, the Bears moved down the field on the accurate passing of Wade and the power running of Ronnie Bull. Reaching the 1-yard line, Bull slanted off-tackle for the Bears' second touchdown of the game. Bob Jencks's extra point put the Bears back in the lead 14–7.

The Steelers' Ed Brown, who had struggled in the early part of the game, began to find his rhythm. Working out of a spread formation, Brown hooked up with Buddy Dial on two completions to move the ball inside Chicago territory. With thirty seconds to play in the half, the Steelers reached the Bears' 31-yard line. Following a time-out, Brown dropped back to pass but could not find anyone open. Forced to move out of the pocket and away from the Bears' pass rush, he spotted Ron Curry breaking open across the middle at the 5-yard line. As Brown threw toward the wide-open Steeler receiver, Roosevelt Taylor instantly broke in Curry's direction. Closing fast, the speedy Bears free safety and the ball arrived in front of Curry at the same time. Taylor, arms extended, leaped to intercept the pass but mistimed his jump. The ball sailed through his arms into the waiting Curry's hands for a Steeler touchdown. Lou Michaels's extra point tied the score at fourteen apiece, as the first half came to a close.

The Steelers had two golden opportunities to take the lead in the third quarter, but Lou Michaels missed two field goals, from 29 and 44 yards. On offense the Bears continued to struggle, as the game remained tied entering the last fifteen minutes of play.

Beginning the fourth quarter the Steelers put a solid drive together off a Bears turnover. Upon reaching the 3-yard line, the Chicago defense held its ground, forcing Pittsburgh to settle for an 11-yard Michaels field goal. There was now just a little more than eight minutes to play in the game, and the Bears trailed 17–14.

The Bears' offense went out onto the field knowing the game was directly on their shoulders. Three pass interceptions and numerous dropped balls had forced them into this do-or-die possession. The Pittsburgh defense had outplayed the Bears' offense all game long. Somehow the Bears would have to find a way to score. The season could depend on it.

In the Bears huddle as Bill Wade began to call a play he glanced at Mike Ditka, who was staring back at him. Ditka had caught six passes for the game, but wanted more. The game was now on the line . . . he wanted the ball. Ditka was about to make one of the greatest runs in Chicago Bear history.

The play was a simple short pass over the middle. Ditka caught the ball and was immediately hit by two Pittsburgh defenders. Refusing to go down, Ditka shook them off, then bowled over another defender and somehow broke away from two other Steelers. Now in the open, running as hard as he could, the big receiver began to tire. Clendon Thomas finally caught him at the 20-yard line, where the exhausted

Ditka carried Thomas forward to the 15-yard line. The play had covered 63 yards, now giving Ditka's team a chance to win the game. Unfortunately, the Chicago offense couldn't capitalize off this great play and settled for an 18-yard field goal. The game was now tied at 17–17.

The Steelers tried to come back, but the now aroused Bears' defense shut them down. Late in the game Wade attempted a pass out in the flat to Joe Marconi. Pittsburgh's John Regar, who was not detected by Wade, stepped in front of Marconi for an easy interception, but the big linebacker dropped the ball. Chicago had escaped a huge mistake that would have easily cost them the game. The final score was 17–17.

On this strange Sunday, when somber crowds gathered at stadiums across the country, the Bears were fortunate just to get a tie. But for Mike Ditka's heroics, the Bears would again be deadlocked with Green Bay in the Western Conference. The Packers had bounced back from their defeat by the Bears last week, defeating San Francisco 28–10. "We were lucky to get a tie, with the way that game went," said a relieved George Halas. "Given the week we have had with all that has happened, it's understandable why we did not play well," he added.

Under the circumstances, this was a game nobody really wanted to play. Somehow the Bears had kept a hold on first place, but now they could not have a loss in the last three games. Everyone on the Bears just wanted to go home, forget football, and pay their proper respects to the late president.

MIKE DITKA (Tight End): "It was my first trip back to Pittsburgh where my parents, my friends, my high school coach, everybody could see me play. It was a very strange event. I remember that Friday when it happened; we were practicing at Wrigley Field. They came out and said that the President has been shot; that's all they said about it. Joe Marconi and I were riding home in a car together when it came on the radio that the President was dead; he had been assassinated. I remember both of us were crying at that time. We went home and, of course, nobody knew what the hell was going on. On Saturday they made the announcement that the games were going to go on. It was very eerie. The media debated whether we should play or not, but I don't think that was the thing . . . I think that Kennedy would have wanted us to play. That was the way I felt. We didn't have any say about it anyway. If the League said 'play,' you played, that's it; that was the end of it. We played the game with a very eerie feeling when we went out onto the field, but once the game started you are playing football. You are trying to beat the other guy's ass; he is trying to beat your ass . . . but a strange game. We could have won it; they could have won it; it ended up being a tie. That tie allowed us to go on to become the champions in 1963."

ROOSEVELT TAYLOR (Defensive Back): "That Pittsburgh game was the saddest game I ever played in. A tie—that's the way it should have been, given the situation. I didn't think we should be playing, but you do what you're told."

ED O'BRADOVICH (Defensive End): "We are not barbarians, you go back through World War I and World War II with the kamikazes. I'm talking about people who don't care about their lives. We are the safest, biggest country, and our own president gets taken out. I was a young man at the time, and when this thing happens, understanding does not come to my mind. What comes to my mind is that a horrific act like that happened, and that is probably why I said somebody should kill the son of a bitch [Oswald]. I recall silence, bewilderment, and going about our business and waiting to hear if we were going to play the game. Those are the three things that come to my mind."

DOUG ATKINS (Defensive End): "In Dallas a few years before, I met Jack Ruby. We went to the Carousel, and I sat there talking politics with him for three hours. He bought the beer, so it was a nice time at his strip joint. Later when he killed Oswald, Stan Jones came up to me and said. 'Doug, that's the guy you were drinking with when we played in Dallas.' I couldn't believe it."

Ronald F. GARVEY

M.D., M.D.A.

In 1953 I began my internship at Parkland Hospital in Dallas, where a few years later I became Resident in Surgery. One of my teammates in college (Harvard) was Ken O'Donnell, who later became a top aide in President Kennedy's administration. We had made arrangements to have lunch with Kenny at the Trade Mart the day that Kennedy came to Dallas in November 1963. While we were waiting for Kenny to arrive, word came that the President had been shot. I got in the car and quickly drove over to Parkland. As I walked into the emergency room, I saw him flat line. They asked me, 'What do we do now, Skip?' I said, 'it doesn't really matter what you do now; when you're dead, you're dead. It does not matter at this point who you are.'

"Just then my brother Jim, who is also a doctor, and Kenny showed up. We went into the nurses' office by ourselves where Kenny placed a call to the White House. I was not the treating physician, but I was right in the middle of it. My brother and a guy named Red Duke initially looked after Governor Connally until some other people showed up. We took care of Mrs. Kennedy who was sitting there with her husband's brain all over her dress, in shock at what had happened. I took the priests to the door— there were two of them—then showed them out the back door. I brought Mrs. Johnson to Mrs. Kennedy so they could talk. I remember I got Mrs. Kennedy a cigarette, which bothered me a bit because I didn't know she smoked. After that, I said, 'Man, I've had all of this I want,' so I left. Theoretically, surgeons are suppose to be tough guys in situations like that, but I just didn't feel like I could do anymore. I thought I'd done a good job, but in retrospect if I had stayed longer, the autopsy possibly would have been done by somebody from Dallas rather than those other people. Maybe it would have been done better, but . . . well, that is just the way I feel about it. I don't have any facts on that. Of course, that was forty years ago.

We were there for twenty-five minutes—the whole goddamned thing took twenty-five minutes. When Lee Harvey Oswald came in, my brother's notes say it was fourteen minutes by the time they got everything done to him in the emergency room and took him to the operating room. Fourteen minutes. When Ruby stuck his gun in his left side, it went through his spleen, his stomach, his liver, and out his right chest. We now call that an LHO, Lee Harvey Oswald. You can't fix that one."

Bears' coaching staff, Halas at the wheel. © Laughead Photographers, courtesy of
Chicago Bears.

Fran Tarkenton. Courtesy of the Minnesota Vikings.

Watch Out!

LITTLE FRAN AND THE VIKINGS
ARE COMING TO TOWN

The week leading up to the rematch with the Vikings was as difficult for the Bears players as it was for everyone else in America. The country was saying good-bye to its slain president, while still trying to get back to some sense of normalcy. The NFL and particularly Commissioner Pete Rozelle had taken some hard hits for playing the games on Sunday. Many writers and fans thought the league was disrespectful to President Kennedy for deciding to play its full schedule of games. Oddly, attendance throughout the league was genuinely good, with few altercations.

PETE ROZELLE (NFL Commissioner): "Everyone has a different way of paying respects. I went to church today as I imagine most people did. I cannot feel that playing the games was disrespectful nor can I feel that I have made a mistake. If I admitted that, I would be saying that playing the games was disrespectful. I do not feel it was so."

For the Bears it was now time to prepare for the Minnesota Vikings. Minnesota always presented a challenge for the Bears, and everyone expected a tough game.

Tackle Stan Jones was settling into his role as a full-time defensive player as the Vikings game approached. Jones, a ten-year veteran, had been selected in the fifth round by the Bears in 1953. Chicago drafted him knowing he would have one more season of eligibility left at the University of Maryland. After a sensational senior year, where he made the All America team, Stan joined the Bears in 1954 and became an immediate starter on the Bears' offensive line. Establishing himself as a premier player, Jones beginning in 1955 was selected to seven consecutive Pro Bowls.

One of the first players to recognize the value of lifting weights (something that was not popular in the early 1950s), he built his 6'1" frame into 260 pounds of muscle.

FRED WILLIAMS (Defensive Tackle): "He was somebody you looked up to. He was one of the strongest people I have ever met. He could lift an opposing lineman up with one arm."

Always a very popular player on the Bears' teams, Stan Jones was selected to be a cocaptain, a position he held for many years.

STAN JONES (Defensive Tackle): "Pete Retzlaff was the president of the Players' Association, and he asked me if he could come to Chicago and speak to the team about joining the players' union. Bill George and I were the captains that year. The Bears didn't belong to the union, and everybody in the league was pissed off at us, because we wouldn't join. The union was asking for fifty dollars a preseason game per player, and we were already getting a hundred dollars. Anyway, Pete said, 'Stan, would you let me come in there and talk to you guys, because if you guys don't join this Players' Association, a lot of the teams have threatened to quit. They are talking about turning it over to the Teamsters or something like that. We will lose control of this association.' 'Well,' I said, 'I don't know if I can get Halas to allow you come in here and speak to the team, but I will talk to him about it.' I went to the old man and told him about Pete wanting to come in and talk with the players about joining the players' union. I said, 'Coach, don't worry about it,' as we had already voted this thing down once before. 'I don't think the guys are going to vote for it.' So he said, 'Well, have your God damned meeting.'

"So Pete came in and did a hell of a sales job. We voted unanimous to join the union. Now I had to go up and tell Halas. I said to Bill

George, 'We have to take the results upstairs to the coach's office.' He said, 'You go up. I'm not going up.' So I went up there. I knocked on the door, and he said, 'Come in.' He took me in the back and said, 'What was the result of your f--king vote?' I said, 'It wasn't my f--king vote. . . . It was the team's vote. We voted unanimously to join the Players' Association.' He said, 'That reflects on the leadership of this team. You're fired!' I got fired from being the captain, and Bill did too. He appointed four new captains. I told Bill afterwards, 'Look at it this way—it took four guys to replace us.' "

"The Minnesota Vikings don't win many games, but they scare the daylights out of almost everybody they play," said George Halas at his weekly press conference. The Vikings, at 4–7, the previous Sunday had beaten the Detroit Lions, 34–31. On offense Minnesota was very dangerous, which was why the Vikings were in most games at the end. Viking quarterback Fran Tarkenton was completing more than 58 percent of his passes, with many of them being thrown to super rookie Paul Flatley. Against Detroit the talented receiver had caught 6 passes for 174 yards. A strong candidate for rookie of the year, he was a dangerous runner after he caught the ball. Flatley, along with Jerry Reichel and Gordy Smith, had formed a good trio of receivers for Tarkenton to throw to. The Minnesota ground attack was also improving, with halfback Tommy Mason ranked third in the NFL in rushing.

On defense the Vikings were struggling, being ranked next to last in points allowed. They had giving up an astonishing 319 points through eleven games this season. The Bears' defense in contrast had given up just 106 points. George Halas hoped his offense would come ready to play against this pathetic defense.

Chicago won the toss and elected to receive. On the third play of the game, the Bears turned the ball over inside their own 20-yard line, as Bill Wade was hit by Minnesota tackle Paul Dixson and fumbled. The Vikings, unable to penetrate the Bears' aroused defense, had Fred Cox come on to kick a 16-yard field goal, to give them the early 3–0 lead.

Late in the first period the Bears' defense turned the tables on the Vikings, when Bill Brown was hit hard by Doug Atkins and fumbled. Roosevelt Taylor, as he had done all season, recovered the loose ball at the Viking 20-yard line. Two minutes later, Roger LeClerc booted a 16-yard field goal to tie the game at three apiece.

Near the end of the first quarter, Minnesota's backup quarterback, Ron Vanderkelen, was forced into service as Tarkenton was injured. The rookie quarterback quickly hooked up with wide receiver Gordy Smith on a couple of great receptions, which placed the ball at the Chicago 2-yard line. On second down, halfback Tom Wilson bolted over the goal line for Minnesota's first touchdown of the game. Fred Cox's kick gave the Vikings a 10–3 lead.

Three minutes later the Vikings shocked the Wrigley Field crowd as Minnesota scored again. Vanderkelen, forced out of the pocket by a big Chicago rush, tossed a short pass to a wide-open Smith near the sidelines. Sidestepping away from Richie Petitbon, Smith had clear sailing to the Bears' goal line. Smith's 53-yard touchdown had stunned the Bears. Cox's point after gave the thirteen-point underdog Vikings a 17–7 lead at halftime.

In the third quarter, the Bears stormed back, going 49 yards on eight plays, with Bill Wade diving over from the 1-yard line. The key play in the drive was a Wade-to-Marconi pass, good for 29 yards. Bob Jencks's extra point cut the Vikings' lead to 17–10.

On the ensuing kickoff, J. C. Caroline hit Minnesota returner Bill Butler so hard that he fumbled the ball, which was recovered by Ed O'Bradovich. Unfortunately, the Bears gave the ball right back, as Galimore fumbled on the next play, after being hit by Viking linebacker Roy Winston.

Trailing by seven points midway through the last quarter, the Bears again were bailed out by their defense. Viking halfback Tommy Mason fumbled at the Minnesota 27-yard line, with Roosevelt Taylor recovering the loose ball. Four plays later, Wade completed a short pass to Marconi for the touchdown. Jencks's kick tied the game at 17–17.

At this point Fran Tarkenton went back into the game, but the aggressive Chicago defense, led by Ed O'Bradovich, pushed the Viking offense back to its own 3-yard line, where they were forced to punt.

A poor punt by Minnesota gave Chicago the ball at the Vikings' 38-yard line. The Bears then drove to the Minnesota 29-yard line where they faced a fourth and one. Halas decided to forego a 36-yard field goal, instead running Ronnie Bull off-tackle. Bull, hit at the line of scrimmage by Winston, in desperation pitched back to a startled Wade, who was immediately sacked by Jim Marshall. The Minnesota defense had perhaps come up with the biggest play of the game.

The Vikings, still unable to move the ball against the stubborn Bears' defense, were again forced to punt. Chicago, now with the ball at their own 24-yard line, with just under a minute to play, ran Bull off-tackle twice to end the game. The Bears walked off the field to a chorus of boos, as the Wrigley faithful were not happy with Halas's decision to settle for the tie.

"Yes, we settled for the tie at the end," said Halas in the Bears' dressing room following the game. Papa Bear had decided that the risk to try to win at the end of the game was not worth it. A tie was better than a loss, as it still would keep the Bears ahead of the Packers. When asked why he didn't try the field goal a few minutes earlier, the Bears' coach said, "We had to go for it, we had momentum. I was sure we would make it, but Winston made a hell of a play. I thought surely we could get within easy field goal range, then win it in the last seconds." Later, when asked if he thought the National Football League should count ties, Halas remarked, "I think the present system is just satisfactory."

Two ties in a row didn't make some of the Bears players happy. "It makes you sick," said defensive captain Joe Fortunato. "We are better than that." Others drew on a much better second-half performance to build on for the upcoming San Francisco game. "We started to play football the second half, instead of pussyfooting around," remarked Bill George.

The Bears, with a half-game lead over the Packers, needed to get back on the winning track. With just two games to go, and the only team to defeat them this season coming to Chicago on Sunday, the Bears had more than enough motivation. San Francisco, this time around, would not be overlooked.

ROGER LECLERC (Kicker): "We were getting beat at halftime. Halas did not like the guys drinking Cokes at halftime. We come in and sit down, and Doug Atkins goes to the cooler and gets a Coke. Halas comes over and says, 'Doug, give me that Coke.' Doug takes the Coke

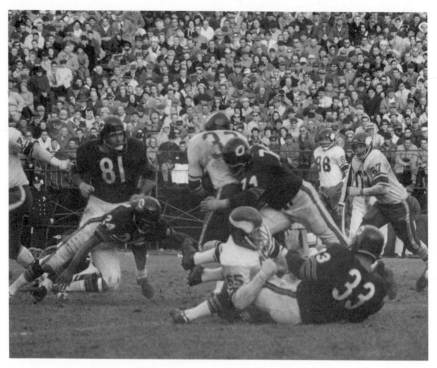

Bob Kilcullen making a tackle against the Minnesota Vikings.
Courtesy of Bob Kilcullen.

and puts it behind him and says, 'You can't have it.' They start arguing back and forth and finally Halas says, 'Doug, look, this is silly. Take one more sip and give me the Coke back.' Doug gives him the Coke back as the referee comes in and informs Halas that there was two minutes to go before the start of the second half. They had argued the whole halftime, and he didn't have a chance to talk to the team."

George Halas and John Johnson stroll along the sidelines. Courtesy of John Johnson.

Willie Galimore. Courtesy of Chicago Bears.

20

Looking for Gold Against Those Pesky 49ers

The NFL held its annual college draft on the Monday following the Minnesota game. Chicago, with the last pick in the first round, selected Tennessee tackle Dick Evey. The Bears announced that Evey on being selected had immediately signed a contract to play for the team next season. Chicago in the second round chose Bill Martin, an end from Georgia Tech. The entire draft would encompass twenty rounds and would be completed in one very long day. The draft order in 1963 was determined by your current record, so the Bears, with the best record in the NFL, chose last.

All playoff information was also released on Monday regarding dates and ticket prices. If the Bears won the Western Conference, they would host the championship game at Wrigley Field on December 29, at 12:05 P.M. Because of the enormous interest in Chicago regarding tickets for the game, the NFL encouraged the Bears to consider moving the game to the much larger Soldier Field, but the Bears decided against it. "Wrigley Field has been the Bears home for 43 years," said George Halas. "And we just would not feel right playing a championship game anywhere else in Chicago." The ticket prices for the game were the following: upper and lower boxes and east stands, $12.50; upper and lower grandstand, $10.00; bleachers, $6.00. Bears season-ticket holders would have first crack at purchasing tickets, but no ticket requests would be accepted by the Bears until the team had clinched the Western Conference.

Chicago, with the tie against the Vikings, remained a half-game ahead of the Packers. The Bears, assuming the Packers won their two remaining games, would have to defeat the 49ers and Lions to win the conference title. Green Bay would finish their season on the West Coast, playing against Los Angeles and San Francisco.

The Eastern Conference entering the thirteenth week of play was also up for grabs. The New York Giants and the Cleveland Browns were tied for first place, with a record of 9–3. The Giants, after winning five games in a row, had struggled the past two weeks, narrowly beating the lowly Dallas Cowboys 34–27 the previous Sunday, after losing to St. Louis the week before. Similar to the Bears, the Giants would be at home for their last two games. The Giants would entertain the Washington Redskins at Yankee Stadium on Sunday, a team they had defeated eleven consecutive times. They would then finish the regular season hosting the dangerous Pittsburgh Steelers. Pittsburgh, in tying Philadelphia last week, was a long shot to win the conference. The Steelers, with a record of 6–3–3, needed to win their remaining two games and needed the Giants, Browns, and Cardinals to all lose theirs. Cleveland, which had won six straight games to begin the season, had to travel to Detroit to play the Lions, then finish up at Washington. The Cardinals, one game back of the Giants and Browns, would also play their last two games at home, first against the Eagles on Sunday, before closing out against Dallas. St. Louis needed both the Giants and the Browns to lose at least one game and needed to win their own remaining two games.

San Francisco, after upsetting the Bears 20–14, had proceeded to lose five out of six games, including their last three. The 49ers, with a record of 2–10, were looking for a couple of upset wins in their last two games against the Bears and Packers.

San Francisco defensive tackle Leo Nomellini was planning to retire after the season, wrapping up a fourteen-year career. "Leo the Lion" was recognized by most experts as one of the greatest players to ever play in the NFL. Drafted in 1950, this 6'3", 265-pound athlete possessed great quickness and strength. Nomellini, who never missed one game in his entire career, was a two-way performer for the 49ers in the mid-1950s, playing both offensive and defensive tackle. A professional wrestler in the off-season, he wrestled the world champion Lou Thesz for the title five times. Nomellini was able to win the championship only once, when Thesz was disqualified for kicking Leo as he tried to climb into the ring. Always serious about his wrestling, if anyone suggested it was staged, Leo would say, "You want to get in the ring with me?" He never had any takers.

On Sunday, the weather was cold and windy, with intermittent sunshine and snow flurries as the players warmed up. The Bears once again lost the coin flip, and went on defense to begin the game. San Francisco, trying to establish the running game, turned the ball over on their first possession when Ed O'Bradovich recovered a Don Lisbon fumble at the Bears' 49-yard line. On first down, Willie Galimore took a Bill Wade handoff, broke through the line, cut hard to his right, then sprinted down the sideline on a 51-yard jaunt for the touchdown. Bob Jenks's kick gave Chicago a 7–0 lead.

The Bears' defense forced another turnover later in the first period, when 49er quarterback Lamar McHan was picked off near midfield by Richie Petitbon. Petitbon stole the ball out of the hands of 49er receiver Monty Stickles, then returned it to the San Francisco 24-yard line. After two running plays netted 5 yards, Joe Marconi, running off-tackle, picked up a great block by tackle Herman Lee and ran untouched into the end zone for the touchdown. Jencks's point after gave the Bears a 14–0 first-quarter lead.

Chicago had another opportunity to extend the lead in the first half, but a poor snap from center prevented a field-goal attempt by Roger LeClerc. Midway through the second quarter another bad snap, this time on a punt, gave the 49ers great field position at the Bears' 26-yard line. San Francisco scored in four plays, as halfback J. D. Smith ran over from the 3-yard line for the touchdown. Tommy Davis's extra point cut the Bears' lead to 14–7. Chicago had outplayed the 49ers on both sides of the ball, but led by only seven point at the half.

The third quarter began with Chicago's Billy Martin returning the San Francisco kickoff to the Bears' 27-yard line, where the 49ers were penalized 15 yards for piling on, moving the ball out to the 42-yard line. Chicago now had excellent field position and struck quickly. Bill Wade went right to the air, completing a 41-yard toss to left end John Farrington, who was brought down at the San Francisco 13-yard line. The Bears reached the 49er 3-yard line where Bill Wade circled the left end for the score. Jencks's third extra point of the game gave the Bears a commanding 21–7 lead.

Lamar McHan, a star in the first game in San Francisco, was harassed the entire game by the Bears' defensive front four. Constantly under pressure, Mchan was finally sent to the sidelines after a vicious hit by Doug Atkins.

The last touchdown of the game was fittingly scored by Chicago's defense. Roosevelt Taylor intercepted a pass headed for receiver Gary Knafelc at the 49ers' 30-yard line. The speedy free safety then bolted back through the San Francisco team for the touchdown. The extra point was blocked. The final score was 27–7.

Chicago had intercepted four San Francisco passes on the day, with Petitbon stealing two and Taylor and Dave Whitsell getting one each. For the season the defense had intercepted thirty-four passes, tying a club record first set in 1941. Both Taylor and Petitbon now had eight interceptions for the year.

In defeating San Francisco, Chicago had improved its record to 10–1–2, which still kept them one-half game ahead of Green Bay, which had won on Saturday, 31–14. The stage was set for the Bears to win their first Western title in seven years. They would have to defeat the Detroit Lions on Sunday. A tie would get the Bears in, but beating Detroit was all George Halas and the players were thinking about.

Roosevelt TAYLOR

DEFENSIVE BACK

The black players stuck together, and the white players stuck together. You understood what the world was about, and you did what you had to do to survive. But there was no extra problems on the Bears.

"Doug Atkins was always so comical in training camp. I can hear him singing, 'On the wings of a snow white dove.' He always spoke his mind. Sometimes he might have said things that were not right, but that's the way he felt. I remember when I came to the Bears I was running punts back. There were two of us deep, Johnny Morris and myself. The guy who didn't field the punt had to block for the other person. Well, I missed my block, and they hammered Johnny. Some of the guys started whispering I was the reason Johnny got hurt. When Doug heard this he came to my defense. He got up one day and said, 'Some of you are saying it's Rosie's fault Johnny got hurt. Well, I'll say this, he's a punt returner, and he shouldn't be in the game if he can't get hurt.' That helped me a lot."

Wrigley Field football scoreboard. © Brace Photo.

21

The Weasel Comes Up Big!

The Bears' approach to their final game of the regular season was first to get the team healthy, then prepare for a difficult game against the Detroit Lions. The Lions, in the midst of a disappointing season, had taken on the role of spoiler in the NFL the past couple of weeks. First, the Lions tied Green Bay on Thanksgiving, 13–13, then delivered a crushing blow to the Cleveland Browns' Eastern-title chances the previous Sunday, by defeating the Browns 38–10.

This traditional season-ending game between the Bears and the Lions over the past few years had been hard fought and tough. In 1962 the Bears had escaped with a 3–0 win, after losing the previous year 16–15. In the 1961 game, Roger LeClerc tied an NFL record with five field goals, but the last-minute heroics of quarterback Earl Morrall saved the day for Detroit. Morrall drove his team 73 yards for a touchdown in the last ninety seconds of the game to defeat the Bears.

Earl Morrall was again back as Detroit's starting quarterback, replacing an inept Milt Plum earlier in the season. The veteran quarterback had thrown for twenty-three touchdowns and was considered by his teammates the Lions' most valuable player. A favorite target of the Detroit quarterback was flanker Terry Barr. Now healthy, he along with Gail Cogdill and Jim Gibbons gave the Lions a talented group of receivers.

On defense Detroit had started slowly in 1963, partly due to the suspension of Alex Karras for gambling. The Lions were playing much better entering the last game of the season, being led by future Hall of Fame players Joe Schmidt and Dick "Night Train" Lane. Schmidt, in his eleventh year with the Lions, was the emotional leader on defense. A seventh-round pick out of the University of Pittsburgh in 1953, he had been selected to the Pro Bowl nine times in his career. The prototype middle linebacker, he and Chicago's Bill George were the premier players at their positions. Schmidt played football with a frenzy, cursing teammates and opponents alike. He was a punishing tackler who had the speed to cover receivers out of the backfield. He loved playing against the Bears, because those games were always rough and hard fought. He thrived on the competition.

ED O'BRADOVICH (Defensive End): "When they made the famous TV documentary *The Violent World of Sam Huff,* they asked Bill George what he thought about *The Violent World of Sam Huff,* and Bill's answer was, 'I don't know too much about that, but if they are really going to do it, they ought to get Joe Schmidt to play the part.' That's the type of respect we all had for Joe Schmidt and the Lions' defense at that time."

Dick "Night Train" Lane began playing in the NFL in 1952, when the Los Angeles Rams signed the former junior-college player to a five thousand dollar contract. An outstanding athlete, he quickly developed into one of the top defensive backs in all of football. Lane in his first season with the Rams set an NFL record for interceptions with fourteen (a record that has lasted more than fifty years).

At 6'2", 210 pounds, he defined the position's toughness with his hard-hitting, aggressive style of play. He was known for the clothesline tackle, which violently hit a receiver around the neck. It was later outlawed by the league. Lane, nicknamed for a popular song of the early 1950s, *Night Train,* was considered by Vince Lombardi to be the best cornerback to ever play the game. He was married to jazz singer Dinah Washington.

Detroit head coach George Wilson, besides trying to derail Chicago's hopes for a conference title, would also be a part of the annual homecoming for former Bear players. A starting right end from

1937 to 1948, Wilson had been a key member of the 1940 team that had defeated the Washington Redskins in the lopsided championship game, 73–0. Regardless of what happened in the Lions and Bears game, Wilson had made plans to attend the Sunday-night banquet with the rest of the former Bear players. The event, hosted by George Halas, might have an interesting twist if the Lions were to upset the Bears.

George Halas decided to give the team Tuesday off from the practice field, allowing many players to have an extra day of rest. Flanker Johnny Morris, who had been held back last week because of a lingering muscle pull, was expected back for the Detroit game. Center Mike Pyle, suffering from an arm injury and groin pull, was hopeful that he could get back to full-time duty. Larry Morris had filled in as the snapper for Pyle against the 49ers, but two high snaps had resulted in the Bears missing one field goal, then not being able to get a punt off. Bears punter Bobby Joe Green had been sacked on the play, giving the 49ers great field position that led to their only score. Another Bears player on the mend was defensive tackle Stan Jones. He had been under the weather with the flu and was just now beginning to get his strength back. "We think the boys being healthy will make a big difference in the game, so an extra day of rest will help all of them," said an understated George Halas.

On Sunday, the Detroit Lions showed up to play the Bears minus two of their key defensive players, Yale Lary and Dick "Night Train" Lane. Lary, who had been suffering from a leg injury, had not recovered sufficiently enough to play. Lane's absence was far more serious. His wife, Dinah Washington, struggling with a weight problem, had died of an accidental overdose of diet pills mixed with alcohol. A grief-stricken Lane remained in Detroit.

Chicago lost the coin toss, and in frigid fifteen-degree weather kicked off to begin the game. Detroit, starting from their own 30-yard line, was shut down on three straight plays, forcing them to punt. Billy Martin, fielding the punt just inside his own 30-yard line, sprinted straight up the field for 5 yards, before he cut sharply toward his left. Martin picked up a block from Bob Wetoska, which gave him running room up the sidelines. Martin, on reaching midfield, sidestepped one

Lion defender, but his foot scraped the sideline chalk. Unaware that he had gone out-of-bounds, Martin sprinted down the field untouched for an apparent Bears touchdown. Wrigley Field exploded with cheers as Martin crossed the goal line, but unfortunately for Bears fans those cheers turned to groans, as the ball was brought back to midfield.

The offense under the direction of Bill Wade picked up a couple of first downs, but a holding penalty forced the Bears to settle for a 19-yard field goal. Chicago took an early 3–0 lead in the game.

Behind the sharp passing of Earl Morrall, the Lions moved back down the field until a Roosevelt Taylor interception in the end zone prevented the Lions from scoring. After an exchange of possessions, the Lions stunned the Chicago faithful on an interception by Larry Vargo. Wade, attempting to complete a pass to Johnny Morris, was picked off by Vargo, who ran 42 yards for a touchdown. Wayne Walkers's extra point gave the Lions a 7–3 halftime lead. Wrigley Field was eerily quiet.

The third quarter began slowly as both teams' defenses dominated the game. On their third possession of the second half the Bears went on the attack, reaching their own 49-yard line. In the huddle Wade looked at Johnny Morris and called "63 sponge." The play was de-signed for the speedy receiver to run 15 yards down the field, then cut sharply across the middle. With Night Train Lane and Yale Lary not in the game, the crafty Morris was taking advantage of Detroit's inexperi-enced defensive backfield. On cue, Morris ran 15 yards, then broke across the middle as Wade released the ball. Lion defender Tom Hall, aware of Morris's speed, had been playing deep and was now trailing Morris on the play. Wade's pass hit a wide-open Morris in stride at the Lion 36-yard line. Hall, still three yards behind, stumbled in his effort to catch the Bears' speedy receiver and fell. Morris turned on the speed and sprinted into the end zone for the score. Bob Jencks's point after gave the Bears a 10–7 lead.

Late in the third quarter, the Bears struck again. The offense back in Lions territory scored when Mike Ditka caught a 22-yard reception in the end zone from Bill Wade. Jencks's kick extended the Bears' lead to 17–7. There were thirty seconds left in the third quarter.

Detroit refused to give up and continued to play the Bears tough.

With just over five minutes remaining in the game, Morrall's short 4-yard toss to receiver Terry Barr brought the Lions within three points of the Bears, 17–14.

The now aroused Detroit defense, to the chagrin of the Bears' fans, shut the Bears down on three straight running plays, forcing them to punt. Bobby Joe Green's booming kick drove Lion returner Tom Watkins back inside the 10-yard line. Quickly moving toward the sideline, Watkins was pushed out-of-bounds at his own 16-yard line. There was now a minute left to play in the game. The Lions still had a chance to win.

On defense, the Bears went with five defensive backs. With the game on the line, George Allen didn't want a repeat of two years ago, when in similar circumstances Morrall had driven his team the length of the field for the victory.

The Bears would give Detroit the short stuff, but no big bombs. The game and the season all came down to these few plays. The Bears' defense, so strong all year, had all the pressure on them to not lose the game.

Defensive back Dave Whitsell broke from the Bear huddle and jogged out to his corner position. One slipup on his part, and the season would be lost. Lined up on the outside . . . the game on the line . . . matched up with a speedy receiver . . . that was what his job was all about. Whitsell took one step back, set his body, took a deep breath, and got ready to make a play.

Earl Morrall dropped back to pass with the intent of finding someone open deep. Detroit, in their double-wing offense, flooded the field with receivers. On the snap Whitsell dropped back 5 yards, providing a safe cushion from which to defend. With each step he moved back, he could see a Detroit receiver coming closer. Whitsell, now backpedaling, changed directions and moved slightly toward the center of the field. Morrall, under heavy pressure from the Bears' front four, turned to avoid being sacked, then heaved the ball deep downfield. Twenty-five yards down the field Whitsell looked up in shock, as the errant pass was headed in his direction. Now changing directions and moving forward, Whitsell had the ball directly in front of him. With palms up, he cradled the ball in his stomach and took dead aim for the Detroit goal line. When he arrived in the end zone, he flung the ball into the stands, to the cheers of a wildly jubilant Wrigley Field crowd, before being mobbed by his teammates. The Bears had done it. They had won the Western Conference. Dave Whitsell was an unlikely hero.

"The Weasel finally got one," said Bears defensive coordinator George Allen. "He chose a most opportune time, and now he is even with the other three." The Bears' coach was referring to Richie Petitbon, Roosevelt Taylor, and Bennie McRae who had all returned interceptions for touchdowns during the season.

George Halas was ecstatic over his team's victory and winning the Western Conference. His Bears had played with a sense of purpose, a renewed desire to be the best. He was as proud of them today as any team in Bears history. Now it was on to the championship game and a date with the New York Giants.

DAVE WHITSELL (Defensive Back): "When I looked up and saw the ball coming toward me I couldn't believe it. I said, 'this one belongs to me.' I caught that ball and headed toward the goal line . . . nobody was going to stop me from scoring that touchdown. What a feeling when I scored and the crowd roared; the stadium just shook. It was something special."

Bob KILCULLEN

DEFENSIVE LINEMAN

I thought when George Allen came in with his enthusiasm and his youth it made all the difference in the world. Clark Shaughnessy was twice his age, so when George came in it was like a breath of fresh air. It wasn't that we didn't get along with Clark, but it was Allen's youth and enthusiasm. I really feel that was what made the defense that year."

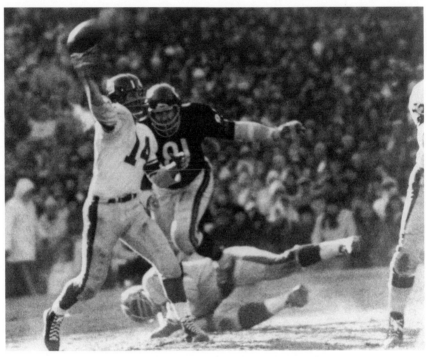

Y. A. Tittle throws downfield as Doug Atkins closes in. Courtesy of Chicago Bears.

22

New York Giants

The New York Giants dispatched the Pittsburgh Steelers 33–17 the previous Sunday to clinch the Eastern Conference title and advance to the championship game against the Bears. This would be the fifth time in six years that New York would be in the final game. The Giants, having lost the past four title games, hoped finally they had the firepower to get past Chicago.

Dating back to 1932, the Bears and Giants had played for the championship five times before. In that first encounter, the Bears prevailed on the outstanding kicking of Jack Manders. "Automatic Jack" was perfect that day, kicking three field goals and two extra points, but the key play of the game was made by Red Grange on defense. As the game came to a close, Grange saved the day when he tackled Giant Dale Burnett, preventing him from scoring the winning touchdown. Each Bears player received $180 dollars for beating the Giants.

A year later the Giants would turn the table and upset the Bears in the famous "Sneaker Game" at the Polo Grounds. Playing on a frozen field, both teams had skidded about in the first half. The Giants came out in sneakers to begin play in the second half and scored twenty-seven points in the last period to upset the previously unbeaten Bears. The teams would meet again for the title in 1941, at Wrigley Field. This time the Bears would be victorious, beating the Giants 37–9. The game was played before only 13,941 fans, due in large part to the U.S. entry into World War II just a few weeks before.

It would be fifteen years before the two teams would play each other again for the title. In 1956, the 9–3 Bears traveled to Yankee Stadium to play the 8–3–1 Giants. Again playing on a frozen field, the Bears wore the wrong type of shoes and got thrashed, 47–7. Seven members from that team were still playing with Chicago in 1963. They included Doug Atkins, Bill George, Fred Williams, Joe Fortunato, Stan Jones, Willie Galimore, and Rick Casares.

STAN JONES (Defensive Tackle): "We had played the Giants in 1956 and lost to them bad in Yankee Stadium. There were a few of us around that still remembered that game. The Giants were the team that got all the publicity. There was a feeling of having something to settle with them."

Each team would again represent its conference in the 1963 World Championship game. The Bears, with a 3–2 lead in title games between the two storied franchises, would have the slight advantage of playing at home.

Predictably, the weather would be cold, with temperatures dipping in the low teens or colder. George Halas took every precaution to have the Wrigley Field turf covered and in the best possible shape for the championship game. Papa Bear did not want a problem with footing. The entire field was covered with a tarpaulin, and then eight tons of hay was distributed over it. This would remain on the field until just a few hours before kickoff. There would be no "Sneaker Game" this year if George Halas had anything to say about it.

As expected, both teams dominated the postseason awards. George Halas was selected coach of the year, and Y. A. Tittle again won the league's MVP Award. Five players from each team were selected to the 1963 All-NFL team. From the Bears, Doug Atkins, Bill George, Joe Fortunato, and Richie Petitbon were selected to the defensive team, while the only Chicago player selected on the offense was Mike Ditka. Mike Pyle, Roosevelt Taylor, and Larry Morris were chosen for the second team. The Giants placed Tittle, Del Shofner, and Roosevelt Brown on offense, with Jim Katcavage and Dick Lynch chosen on defense. Giants middle linebacker Sam Huff earned second-team honors.

The Bears, placing four players on the All-NFL defensive team, were not satisfied that more of their defensive team were not selected. "Larry Morris should have made first team," said Dave Whitsell. "But you know how it is, we have already got two linebackers there, so everyone thinks that is enough from one team." Morris was just happy to be considered. Originally drafted by the Los Angeles Rams, he suffered through four injury-plagued seasons with them, before being traded to Washington. Morris, in a contract dispute, refused to report to the Redskins and was dealt to the Bears for a second-round pick. In five years with Chicago, he had never missed a game. He was looking forward to the game against the Giants. "They have a good team, but we're better," he said. "We will win."

George Halas rewarded his team, giving them three full days off following the Detroit game. It would be two weeks before the Giants and Bears would do battle, so Halas would use the extra time to watch film with his staff, then prepare a game plan.

GEORGE HALAS (Owner/Head Coach, Chicago Bears): "Football is so much more complicated today than it was in the old days, even though the basic requirements are still good blocking and tackling. All the coaches spend hours going over game movies. The defenses are so much stronger now. In the old days we used to spend one day a week on defense, now it's 50–50, offense and defense."

A typical day for the Bears' coach would be to arrive at the Bears' office at 9:00 A.M. for a three-hour meeting with the coaches. A short meeting with the players would begin at 12:30, followed by practice on the field. After practice, he would watch film until 4:30 P.M. Halas then would return to the Bears' office to conduct a strategy meeting with his staff, until around nine o'clock. Home for a late dinner with his wife, he would read the paper and go to bed. This was a routine he would maintain all season.

The potent Giant offense was a big concern to the Bears' defensive guru, George Allen. He and his staff had been working overtime, breaking down the Giants' plays and deciding on the types of coverage to use. Allen wanted to know exactly what the Giants would do on each play, based on field position, the game situation, and length of yards needed for a first down. Every play was dissected. It was his goal to have his defense prepared for everything the Giants would throw at them. Allen would have his team so schooled on the Giants that each time the Giants came to the line of scrimmage, his team would instantly know the formation. He and his staff would work around the clock to accomplish this.

Yelberton Abraham Tittle had just set an NFL record of thirty-six touchdown passes in 1963, breaking his old record by two, set a year earlier. Tittle, at thirty-seven years old, just seemed to get better each year. The native Texan utilized all his receivers and could throw long or short with precision. He and his star receiver Del Shofner had hooked up on nine touchdown passes for the year, with an average completion of 18.5 yards per catch. Veteran halfback Frank Gifford was now being used almost exclusively as a flanker, catching forty-two passes for seven touchdowns. Also becoming a reliable receiver out of the backfield was halfback Phil King, who had caught thirty-two passes, while rushing for a team-high 613 yards. Longtime Giants Joe Morrison and Alex Webster were still effective players, but their roles had been diminished in 1963. Joe Walton at tight end had caught twenty-six passes, but because of a leg injury, his availability for the championship game was questionable. If Walton could not play, he would be replaced by Aaron Thomas, a talented young player who had three touchdown receptions on twenty-two catches.

STAN JONES (Defensive Tackle): "Some writer asked Dave Whitsell how he thought he would do against Del Shofner. Dave said, 'I will shut him out!' Dave was a character—what he lacked in talent, he made up with self-confidence."

NBC had the contract to televise the championship game, investing a record $926,000 for the broadcast rights. Because the NFL policy blocked out all coverage within a seventy-five-mile radius of the game, the city of Chicago would not receive the broadcast. Commissioner Pete Rozelle, in a failed attempt to get the Bears to move the game to the larger Soldier Field, decided to offer a closed-circuit broadcast of the game to Chicago football fans.

Three local arenas with a combined seating capacity of 25,500 seats were leased to Theatre Network Television, better known as TNT. The locations chosen for the viewing were McCormick Place, the International Amphitheater, and the Chicago Coliseum. Ticket prices would range from $4.00 to $7.50 dollars each. All tickets would be on a reserved basis, and the game would be shown on a screen of 700 square feet, approximately twice the size of a typical theater screen in 1963. The new modern cameras would reportedly allow the fans to "follow the ball and see each play as never before on commercial TV." The rumor leading up to the game was that the NFL would eventually abandon commercial television for this new pay-per-view idea.

On December 29, 1963, a bright, cold, sunny day in Chicago, the Giants and the Bears took the field to decide who would be crowned the best team in professional football. This classic matchup of an irresistible force, the Giants' offense, versus the immovable object, the Bears' defense, had all the ingredients for a great game. The contest, on paper too close to call, went off at 6–5 odds, you pick them.

The temperature, hovering around eight degrees, quickly froze the field when the tarpaulin and hay were removed. The players, besides the bone-chilling cold, would have to play the game on a slick field.

The Bears won the toss and elected to receive. The offense reached their own 41-yard line, when Bill Wade on a quarterback option was hit from behind by Dick Lynch and fumbled, with the ball being recovered by the Giants' Erich Barnes. On an assortment of screen passes and running plays, New York quickly moved inside the Bears' 15-yard line. Tittle faked a dive to his halfback, Phil King, then as he was being hit by Larry Morris, he lofted a pass to the corner of the end zone to Frank Gifford for the touchdown. Don Chandler's point after gave the Giants an early 7–0 lead, but the Giants' quarterback noticeably limped off the field.

Near the conclusion of the first quarter, the Bears turned the ball over again, when Willie Galimore fumbled at the Bears' 31-yard line. Tittle, going right to the air, hit a wide-open Del Shofner in the end zone with a perfect pass. Shofner, who had caught many passes like this all year, dropped the ball. Tittle, confident now that the Bears would aggressively rush him, attempted a screen pass to Phil King. The Bears' Larry Morris stepped in front of King and intercepted the ball. With no Giants in his way, Morris set off for the New York goal line. Reaching the Giants' 6-yard line, he was pulled down from behind by Darrell

Dess and Greg Larson. The Bears linebacker had rumbled 61 yards on the play. After the huge play by Morris, Chicago wasted no time scoring as Bill Wade dove over from the 2-yard line. Bob Jencks's extra point tied the game at 7–7.

RONNIE BULL (Halfback): "Larry Morris set up our first touchdown with the pass interception and ran for 60 yards. He tells the great story that the first 30 yards he was afraid they were going to catch him, and the last 30 yards he was afraid they were not."

Undaunted, Tittle drove the Giants back down the field, highlighted by a 36-yard pass to Aaron Thomas. The Giants pushed inside the Bears' 3-yard line, but three incomplete passes by Tittle brought Chandler back on the field for the easy field-goal try. Chandler split the uprights to put the Giants back on top 10–7.

New York, regaining the ball after the Bears punted, tried to quickly move back down the field. Attempting a sideline pass to Gifford, Tittle was again hit hard in the knee by Larry Morris. Immediately falling to the ground, Tittle was helped off the field as the first half came to a close.

In the locker room, the Giants' quarterback was in tremendous pain and had the New York trainers shoot him with novocaine and cortisone. Tittle warmed up on the Giant sidelines to begin the second half with his knee heavily bandaged.

Late in the third quarter, from his own 38-yard line, Tittle attempted another screen pass, this time to Joe Morrison. Chicago's Ed O'Bradovich intercepted the ball and returned it to the Giants' 14-yard line, giving the Bears great field position. The Bears ran two plays inside, but the Giants' defense held them to just 2 yards. On third down Bill Wade found reliable Mike Ditka open at the 10-yard line. Catching the ball, Ditka dragged Giant defender Dick Pesonen to the 1-yard line. On the next play Wade dove into the end zone for the touchdown. The Bears, off O'Bradovich's great play, had forged into the lead, 14–10.

The Giants gamely tried to come back late in the game. Tittle completed three passes, the last to Frank Gifford, which gave the Giants a first down at the Bears' 36-yard line. With time running out, Tittle threw deep to his favorite target, Del Shofner. The ball was over-

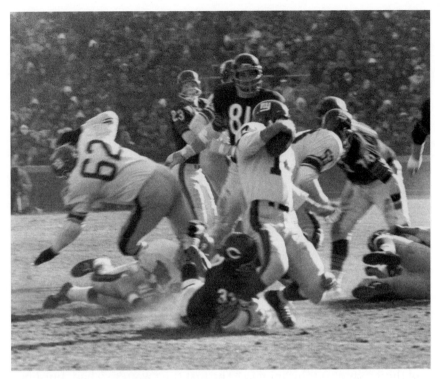

Larry Morris (33) sacks the Giants' Y. A. Tittle (14) in Championship Game.
Courtesy of Chicago Bears.

thrown and soared over Shofner's head into the waiting arms of Richie
Petitbon. The Bears had won the championship.

Chicago fans surged onto the field to celebrate their team's victory.
The immovable object had done just enough to survive this hard-
fought game. The Chicago Bears were the World Champions for the
eighth time.

In the Bears' locker room George Halas was relieved after his team's
win. "It wasn't easy. I didn't think it would be," Halas said. "This was
great, just great. I would have to rank this up with the 73–0 win over the
Redskins." When asked if he would now retire after winning this championship, the Bears' coach remarked, "I may have something to say
about that after the Pro Bowl, but with us playing the College All-Stars
next year in Chicago, I might have to come back for that. Besides where
is a 68-year-old man going to find another job anyway?"

Larry Morris was awarded the Most Valuable Player Award by *Sport Magazine,* which meant he won a brand-new Chevrolet Corvette. To a man, the players decided that the game ball should go to George Allen. The young coach, through his hard work and dedication, had transformed this Bears defense into one of the finest to ever play the game. Standing there holding the game ball, Allen offered insights into his team's approach: "We had to destroy Tittle's accuracy as best we could, then leave it to the secondary to pick off the passes that went astray. Five interceptions today, that makes 41 for the year. That's a remarkable accomplishment." Indeed it was.

The Bears players would receive $6,000 each for winning the title. The Giants' share would be $4,200. Over in the New York locker room, Allie Sherman defended his quarterback's five interceptions. "Anybody who says Y.A. Tittle can't come up with the big game and can't produce under pressure, doesn't know anything about football. I couldn't find another quarterback who could have handled us any better. He got hurt. . . . He got hurt badly but still played."

Tittle, whose injury was described as twisted ligaments of the knee, had this to say about his injury: "The first time wasn't so bad, but I had to go back out there. It was my decision to play. I sort of felt like I needed to give it a good try." Unable to move well, his heroic attempt at playing didn't escape his teammates. "It took a heck of a man to do what he did today," said center Jack Stroud. "He couldn't run, that's why he wasn't up to par. It threw his passing off. Usually he does not need much time. He throws quickly but with a bad leg he had to take longer. It took him longer to get in the drop back position."

LARRY MORRIS (Linebacker): "When I came out of the game George Halas hugged me. One of our assistant coaches came up to me afterwards and said, 'Larry, you're the first player I have ever seen Coach Halas hug.' Before the game Fred Williams, Bill George, and I had a pool where we said if any of us should win the MVP, we would share the award, which was a brand-new Corvette. When I won it I had to give Fred and Bill a thousand dollars each."

ED O'BRADOVICH (Defensive End): "We were in a basic 4–3 defense. The Giants had got to the championship game using 'lates' [play-action plays] and 'screens.' They were a great screening team and they would come with the play action, and that is what got them to the championship game. Tittle in that offense had passed for a bizillion yards that year. We knew all their tendencies. If they sneezed, George Allen knew about it. This particular play, Joe [Fortunato] called the defense and then he said, 'Where they'll beat us is when they screen,' which I knew because of all the studying I did. Joe says, 'Just watch for the screen.' At the snap of the ball, my man [Jack Stroud] kind of engaged me, but weakly. You could just read it—he didn't set up and then fire at you, he just kind of drifted back. You can tell what an offensive tackle is going to do with how much tension they have on their arm when they are in three-point stance. I just planted my right foot, and I remember I went out into the flat. Lo and behold, Tittle drops back, throws the ball, and I snatch it with my left hand and that was it. But the fact of the matter was we *knew* it was coming."

JOE FORTUNATO (Linebacker): "We had a pretty good tendency chart on the Giants. We followed that chart. They did just about what George Allen had predicted they would do, based on their past tendencies. What I'm saying is they would do certain things in certain situations. We just followed that all the way through the game. A good example was O'Bradovich's interception. We called it in our huddle.

"Everybody was talking about a screen because that was a situation where they liked to screen a lot. Again, that was part of knowing the tendencies of what they tended to do, being prepared."

ERICH BARNES (Defensive Back, New York Giants): "The Bears couldn't move on us, and we couldn't move on them. When Tittle got hurt we should have called three running plays and punted when we were in the lead. That was a funny game because I was playing against my former team, guys I liked and respected. Against the Bears we felt we were head-and-shoulders better on offense than the Bears. Now the defense we felt was a standoff, because we were both good. Of course, when you play a game in the dead of winter everything is neutralized. We had the game won before it had started. We had the lead, and Shofner drops one in the end zone—he was wide open. Then the game unfortunately takes another turn."

BILL WADE (Quarterback): "I always refer to the championship game as the 'Big Game.' I mean, here we had worked so hard to get

Ed O'Bradovich (87) makes a key interception against the Giants in the
1963 Championship Game. Courtesy of Chicago Bears.

where we wanted to get. We knew that it would be an exciting game
and that the crowd would be for us, but when you're out on the field,
it is just who wants to block and who wants to tackle. Unfortunately,
when the field is like it is, it made for another thing. When I ran the ball
the first time, a quarterback draw to the right and I was going down
field and just making a fake outside and cutting inside when a guy

knocked the ball out from behind. I don't even know today who it was. Somebody just knocked the ball out of my arms from behind. I had made about ten yards. We knew the Giants defense was coordinated in a way that Sam Huff was going one way or the other, based on the formation we were in. If we send two men to the left for instance, our left, Huff, would go to the left. That meant if you could split the defensive end and the defensive tackle, I had a pretty good running lane. That is where I was able to make some good yardage during the game. We were definitely prepared for the Giants that day, and it paid off in a World Championship for our team and fans."

MIKE DITKA (Tight End): "That championship game was cold. I don't think it was any colder than the Detroit game, but it was cold. I thought we had played the game awfully close to the vest offensively; we didn't really open it up at all. We just did the things we always did, and our defense just hung in there and fought with them. They just shot them down. They had one chance for a big play when Shofner dropped the ball in the end zone because he slipped. Other than that it was just a slugfest. We averaged giving up ten points a year on defense and on offense we averaged about 14 points a game. That was the final score of the game, 14–10. That's a fact."

Doug Atkins Day. *Rear (left to right):* Mike Timmlin, Doug Atkins, Bill Wade, Maury Youmans, Joe Fortunato, Ed McCaskey, Biff George, George Conner. *Front (left to right):* Stan Jones, Ted Karras, Ronnie Ball, Bob Kilcullen, Larry Morris, Mike Ditka. Courtesy of Doug Atkins.

23

More Stories from the Locker Room

"When you get too old to set a bad example, you might as well give some good advice."
—Chuck Mather, coach

MIKE DITKA (Tight End): "The Bears in 1985 were a very good football team. Buddy Ryan had a system; it was the 46 defense. You basically are coming with eight men up front. You're playing an 8-3; that's what you're playing. You still have man-to-man on the corners all the time, and that one free man must be near the line of scrimmage to pick up any back or anything else that comes out. The rest are coming. Now, some of them are coming on the Red Dog where they might have a peel off assignment, but they are coming. We played that system, and we had the people who could play that system. That was a great defense, but the defense in 1963 did not play gimmick games. Yes, we would drop down into a five man front once in awhile, and we probably did a few more things than most teams did, but basically it was 'no gimmicks.' It was just people playing football. I'm not sure our defense man-to-man in 1963 wasn't a better defense personnelwise."

JOE FORTUNATO (Linebacker): "Pittsburgh had us 17–10 right at the end of the ball game. Mike Ditka caught a pass over the middle, and he ran for a touchdown. He must have run over ten guys. It tied the game, and that's how we won that championship—by one-half game—and that was it right there."

MIKE DITKA (Tight End): "I think the greatest play of the season for me was when Davey Whitsell picked out the pass and went for a touchdown against Detroit. That was the best. Then we knew we were in the championship game."

MIKE PYLE (Center): "Football is the greatest team game there is. No one ever accomplishes something by themselves. The entertainment factor has allowed that to change today. A guy that scores a touchdown now thinks he's the guy that did it. They forget there are eleven guys, but no one cares. I mean, what the hell . . . do your thing. I want to watch it, but, frankly, the game isn't as good."

MAURY YOUMANS (Defensive End): "When I was a rookie Bill George always scared the hell out of me. I remember later that year he came up and sat next to me on the plane. He in his way gave me a pat on the back. He said, 'You're going to get better. The more you're in this league, you're going to get better.' That meant a lot to me, especially coming from him, because he was our leader."

ANGELO COIA (Flanker): "My rookie year I had bought a new car—it was a convertible. We were practicing at Soldier Field. Now I don't know if Halas was mad at me or what for having this new car. I had the top down and we're practicing, and this storm is blowing in off Lake Michigan. I asked him if I could put the top up on my car. He said, 'You're not going to put the top up on that c--t wagon,' he said. 'Let it fill up with water.' And it did—it was like a bathtub."

CHUCK MATHER (Coach): "Doug Atkins physically was the greatest athlete of that particular time. He had the size and more ability than the rest of them. The thing about Doug is he didn't like to work. He liked to play, but he didn't like to practice. Particularly when he got older, he'd be on the sideline watching practice."

MIKE PYLE (Center): "One of Halas's ways to get guys not to eat and not to drink was to lower their assigned weight. He had been doing it that way for a long time so you weren't going to change him, but it destroyed a great football player in Herman Lee, and it did with some others."

JOE FORTUNATO (Linebacker): "Clark Shaughnessy put us at a disadvantage in one sense, but he had one of the best minds, football minds, that I have ever known. He just tried to do too much. He was putting the linebackers over the offensive guards, which at times made it hard for the linebackers to cover the backs. Some of the things he did were just too tough to do."

MIKE PYLE (Center): "It wasn't that the training staff was incompetent. It was the control that Halas had over the doctors and their decisions. Freddy Williams told me that he never found out that he had a cracked rib or a broken bone until much later on—they never told him. The only place we ever had physicals was at camp with Halas's old navy buddy from Milwaukee."

ED O'BRADOVICH (Defensive End): "I hate to think of how many shots of cortisone I got over the years from Dr. Fox. Maybe you should take one shot a year. I was getting maybe two, three, four, maybe six shots a week. We did what the old man dictated, and basically that was the way the NFL was then."

MAURY YOUMANS (Defensive End): "I had twenty-one shots in my back one year."

MIKE PYLE (Center): "I had to be shot up for the last three games and the championship game against the Giants. I had both groin muscles shot up with a spinal needle—it was about three or four inches long. You are playing for a championship, you don't even think about it. I told them I want to play.

"Larry Morris had torn his knee up, and he kept getting shots in it to get through the season. When they went to operate, it was all ground up. The whole cartilage was nothing but dust."

MAURY YOUMANS (Defensive End): "Normally on a knee operation you are back in six weeks. I had an infection that whole year. It used to leak. I would wear big bandages when I went to bed, and they would be soaked when I got out of bed."

MIKE PYLE (Center): "A guy dislocates an elbow today, and the game stops for twenty minutes. I dislocated an elbow and got up and

Old Bears get together a few years after the championship to reminisce. *Left to right:*
Ed O'Bradovich, Fred Williams, Doug Atkins, and Bill George. Courtesy of Biff
George.

ran off the field. You get off the field. I wasn't going down. I was going
to get off the field as best I could."

ROOSEVELT TAYLOR (Defensive Back): "I intercepted a pass
in the end zone. I was running it back. A couple of guys took shots at
me but missed. I'm on about the 15-yard line, and I'm seeing a 105 interception return. Out of nowhere comes the Lions' tight end Gibbons. He hit me so hard as I didn't see him coming that everybody
gasped. I fumbled the ball, but I managed to fall on it. Man, that was
some hit."

MIKE PYLE (Center): "I would go to George Halas, representing
the team, and had probably a little different relationship than, say, a guy
representing himself. I had a tendency to want to represent the team. I
found him to be very paternalistic as opposed to businesslike. That pa-
ternalism is where I think George Halas created some animosity among
some players. I'll give you an example about the paternal. Let's say a fa-

ther has five boys. The ones that are the most accomplished take care of themselves and don't get much attention from the father. The boys that were problems, boys that had some problems, the father takes care of them. That's the way I looked at what George Halas did with our team. Some guys like Stan Jones, who would do anything for the old man and the team, were never rewarded. Others who were a constant pain to him, he would take care of them. The troublemakers were rewarded, and the supportive guys generally weren't."

MAURY YOUMANS (Defensive End): "The Cottage (Chicago restaurant) had an ice statue of a bear one year. Doug Atkins put this big salami on the bear and couldn't wait till the players brought their wives in and show them that bear. One of the wives said, 'That's not so big.' That poor guy got razzed hard in the locker room the rest of the year."

LEO GEORGE (Bill George's son): "My father and Fred Williams went to this speaking engagement together. After it was over this guy hands my father an envelope with money. My dad hands it to Fred and says, 'Go in the bathroom and see how we did.' So Fred goes into the bathroom and there was six fifty-dollar bills in there. So Fred takes out one fifty-dollar bill, seals the envelope back up, and went back outside. So, my dad said, 'How did we do?' Fred says, 'I couldn't tell you, because someone walked in, just as I was ready to count the money,' and hands the envelope back to my father. My dad goes in the bathroom and comes back out, and Fred says, 'How did we do?' My father says, 'Do you believe the son of a bitch only gave us two hundred dollars!' "

MIKE PYLE (Center): It wasn't a matter of money back then, it was the privilege of playing. That sounds silly in this day and age, but I looked at it as a privilege to have been a part of the Chicago Bears and to have met the individuals I met in my career.

MIKE DITKA (Tight End): "There were four teams that talked to me before the draft, Pittsburgh, San Francisco, Washington, and Chicago. If I had played for Pittsburgh, San Francisco, or Washington I would have been a linebacker. The only team that I would have been a tight end with was the Bears. The reason was Halas. I don't think he ever got the credit he deserved for what he did. He really is the one

Media guide, 1964. Courtesy of Chicago Bears.

who created the tight end position . . . not me. Halas and Luke (Johnsos) figured out how to use a tight end. They knew you were going to get coverage by a linebacker or safety. Then when I had trouble getting off the line, they split me out where the linebacker gave me a two-way release instead of a one-way release."

Epilogue

The New York Giants and Chicago Bears would not return to the championship game in 1964, with both teams having very disappointing seasons. The Giants would fall to the bottom of the Eastern Conference with a record of 2–10–2. Injuries and age would take its toll, as the once powerful Giant offense ranked next to last in points scored. Thirty-eight-year-old Y. A. Tittle, in his final season in the NFL, would throw for only ten touchdowns, some twenty-six fewer than a year before. Star receiver Del Shofner would get injured and play in only six games, catching no touchdown passes. The Giants would slip into mediocrity the remainder of the decade.

The Bears' celebration as World Champions came crashing to a sudden halt the following year in training camp. Sadly, Willie Galimore and John Farrington were killed in an automobile accident while returning to camp. Their sudden loss devastated the team. The two players were at practice one day, then dead the next. Both were very popular among their teammates, and the team lost its focus from then on.

GEORGE HALAS (Coach): "One evening during our 1964 training camp, Willie Galimore and John Farrington were absent when our eight o'clock chalk talk was due to begin. They had gone out for a couple of quick beers. I delayed the class to their return. Then came a

Bob Kilcullen tackles Don Perkins in a 1964 game against the Dallas
Cowboys. Courtesy of Bob Kilcullen.

dreadful phone call. The two Bears on their return to camp missed a
sharp turn on the highway. Their car had crashed into a barn killing
both instantly. The tragedy blotted out enthusiasm carried over from
our 1963 championship. For the Bears, our season was over before it
began."

Also, a big problem in 1964 was George Halas's refusal to give
players a proper raise for winning the championship. The players felt

Halas betrayed them by not rewarding them for such a great season. Many players stayed out of training camp that year in deference to Halas's penny-pinching ways. The Bears would tumble to a record of 5–9, finishing next to last in the conference. The defense, so great in 1963, never played with the same fire again.

Maury Youmans was traded to the Dallas Cowboys in the off-season, where he started at defensive end for two years before retiring from football in 1966.

Mike Pyle. © Brace Photo.

Mike PYLE

CENTER

You know, it was a funny thing when we played in the '60s. . . . We thought we were being paid to play! They don't think that anymore because of the money. Players call their agents before they go to see the trainer and ask, 'When should I get well?' All of that bullshit with the amount of money they're paid. How arrogant the things they do. My answer has always been the same, 'Back when I played in the '60s, I thought they paid me that little bit of money to play, so I played.' It is different today."

1963 NFL Final Standings

EASTERN CONFERENCE

	Won	Lost	Tie	PF	PA
New York Giants	11	3	0	440	280
Cleveland Browns	10	4	0	343	262
St. Louis Cardinals	9	5	0	341	283
Pittsburgh Steelers	7	4	3	321	295
Dallas Cowboys	4	10	0	305	378
Philadelphia Eagles	2	10	2	242	381
Washington Redskins	3	11	0	279	398

WESTERN CONFERENCE

	Won	Lost	Tie	PF	PA
Chicago Bears	11	1	2	301	144
Green Bay Packers	11	2	1	369	206
Baltimore Colts	8	6	0	316	285
Minnesota Vikings	5	8	1	309	390
Detroit Lions	5	8	1	326	265
Los Angeles Rams	5	9	0	210	350
San Francisco 49ers	2	12	0	198	391

Third-Place Game: Cleveland Browns 23, Green Bay Packers 40
Championship Game: New York Giants 10, Chicago Bears 14

1963 NFL Championship Game

DECEMBER 29, 1963

					Total
Chicago	7	0	7	0	14
New York	7	3	0	0	10

FIRST QUARTER

N.Y.   Gifford, 14-yard pass from Tittle (Chandler kick)

Chi.   Wade, 2-yard run (Jencks kick)

SECOND QUARTER

N.Y.   Chandler, 13-yard field goal

THIRD QUARTER

Chi.   Wade, 1-yard run (Jencks kick)

FOURTH QUARTER

No scoring

Team Statistics

	Chicago	N.Y.
First Downs—total	14	17
Punts—number	7	4
Punts—average distance	41.0	43.3
Punt Returns—yards	5	21
Interception Returns—number	5	0
Interception Returns—yards	71	0
Fumbles—number	2	2
Fumbles—lost	2	1
Penalties	5	3
Yards Penalized	35	25

Individual Statistics

Chicago	ATT	YDS	AVG
Bull	13	42	3.2
Wade	8	34	4.3
Galimore	7	12	1.7
Marconi	3	5	1.7
Totals	31	93	3.0

New York	ATT	YDS	AVG
Morrison	18	61	3.4
King	9	39	4.3
McElhenny	7	19	2.7
Webster	3	7	2.3
Tittle	1	2	2.0
Totals	38	128	3.4

RECEIVING

Chicago	NO	YDS	AVG
Marconi	3	64	21.3
Ditka	3	38	12.7
J. Morris	2	19	9.5
Coia	1	22	22.0
Bull	1	-5	-5.0
Totals	10	138	13.8

New York	ATT	YDS	AVG
Gifford	3	45	15.0
Morrison	3	18	6.0
Thomas	2	46	23.0
McElhenny	2	20	10.0
Webster	1	18	18.0
Totals	11	147	13.4

PASSING

Chicago	ATT	COMP	YDS	INT
Wade	28	10	138	0

New York	ATT	COMP	YDS	INT
Tittle	29	11	147	5
Griffing	1	0	0	0